The Mindfulness-Based Emotional Balance Workbook

An Eight-Week Program For Improved Emotion Regulation And Resilience

Margaret Cullen, MA, MFT
Gonzalo Brito Pons, PhD

EasyRead Large

Copyright Page from the Original Book

Distributed in Canada by Raincoast Books

Copyright © 2015 by Margaret Cullen and Gonzalo Brito Pons
New Harbinger Publications, Inc.
5674 Shattuck Avenue
Oakland, CA 94609
www.newharbinger.com

Excerpt from "With that Moon Language" by Hafiz from A YEAR WITH HAFIZ: DAILY CONTEMPLATIONS, by Hafiz, translated by Daniel Ladinsky. Copyright © 2010 Daniel Ladinsky. Used by permission of Daniel Ladinsky and Penguin Publishing Group. All rights reserved.

Excerpt from Thich Nhat Hanh's "Adjusting Posture," in chapter 5, from STEPPING INTO FREEDOM: AN INTRODUCTION TO BUDDHIST MONASTIC TRAINING by Thich Nhat Hanh, translated by Annabel Laity. Copyright © 1997 Thich Nhat Hanh. Used by permission of Parallax Press.

Cover design by Amy Shoup; Acquired by Catharine Meyers; Edited by Ken Knabb

Library of Congress Cataloging-in-Publication Data

Cullen, Margaret (Margaret Anne), 1952-
 The mindfulness-based emotional balance workbook : an eight-week program for improved emotion regulation and resilience / Margaret Cullen, MA, MFT, and Gonzalo Brito Pons, PhD.
    pages cm
 Includes bibliographical references.
 ISBN 978-1-60882-839-5 (paperback) -- ISBN 978-1-60882-840-1 (pdf e-book) -- ISBN 978-1-60882-841-8 (epub)
1. Mind and body therapies. 2. Mental health. 3. Self-management (Psychology) I. Brito Pons, Gonzalo. II. Title.
RC489.M53C85 2015
616.89--dc23
                        2015005422

TABLE OF CONTENTS

"In an increasingly topsy-turvy world, finding emotional balance is more important than ever—and Margaret Cullen and Gonzalo Brito Pons show you how, walking with you step-by-step, drawing on brain science, ancient wisdom, and the power of mindfulness. Comforting and powerful, down-to-earth and profound, this book is a clear path from stress, frustration, and irritation to calm strength, happiness, and inner peace."

—**Rick Hanson, PhD,** author of *Buddha's Brain*

"Bravo to *The Mindfulness-Based Emotional Balance Workbook!* This is a very wise and compassionate book that shows how you can transform difficult emotions by acknowledging and embracing them as a path to greater freedom and peace."

—**Bob Stahl, PhD,** coauthor of *A Mindfulness-Based Stress Reduction Workbook, Living with Your Heart Wide Open, Calming the Rush of Panic, A Mindfulness-Based Stress Reduction Workbook for Anxiety,* and *MBSR Every Day*

"*The Mindfulness-Based Emotional Balance Workbook* combines the wisdom of reflection, the beauty of compassion, and the rigor of science. It guides its readers into the capacity of mindfulness to reduce emotional reactivity and cultivate kindness, compassion, and forgiveness. The wealth of ideas and practices in this illuminating work will be of benefit and has the potential to transform our individual and collective lives."

—**Shauna Shapiro, PhD,** professor at Santa Clara University and author of *The Art and Science of Mindfulness* and *Mindful Discipline*

"It is the nature of the human condition to suffer. For many their suffering is worsened by negative emotional states. Using not only their extensive experience as mindfulness teachers but also the knowledge gained by working with leading emotion researchers, the authors give a step-by-step road map to improve one's resilience and create emotional balance that is accessible to all. For anyone living in today's rushed and stressful world, this book is a must-read."

—**James R. Doty, MD,** professor of neurosurgery and founder and director of the Center for Compassion and Altruism Research and Education at Stanford University School of Medicine

"This wise and practical book is filled with wonderful practices that can regulate your emotions and change your life."

—**Jack Kornfield, PhD,** author of *The Wise Heart*

"Like other animals, humans evolved with a range of complex emotions that can be sources of joy but also pain and suffering. Unlike other animals though, humans have a capacity for being aware of, observing, and mindfully choosing how to work with these passions of the mind. In this beautifully accessible and carefully crafted book two leading mindfulness teachers have come together to guide us through the sometimes stormy terrain of our emotions. This step-by-step eight-week course is rich in insights and skillfully organized practices for working with and cultivating our minds. Based on the most up-to-date research, this book is a gift for all those seeking emotional balance in the hustle-bustle of modern-day life."

—Paul Gilbert, PhD, FBPsS, OBE, Derbyshire Healthcare NHS Foundation Trust Mental Health Research Unit, Kingsway Hospital

"Seamlessly integrating the twin curricula of mindfulness meditation and emotion science, this pragmatic and wise workbook provides readers with clear-sighted guidance for self-care when distressing effects loom."

—Zindel V. Segal, PhD, distinguished professor of psychology in mood disorders, University of Toronto Scarborough

"This is an extraordinary book that brings together science, Dharma, and psychology in an accessible, actionable, practical, and inspiring way. Not only is this book a must-read but also a 'must-use' in a time on our planet where there is so much stress and suffering. Margaret and Gonzalo have done a great service in crafting approaches to emotional balance based on the work of Drs. Paul Ekman and Alan Wallace, as well as their years of practice and study."

—Roshi Joan Halifax, Abbot, Upaya Zen Center

"At last! A truly useful application of mindfulness to managing the emotional storms of everyday life. This eight-step program helps readers steadily change their relationship to their emotions, becoming less reactive and more flexible. The authors unpack the deep wisdom of Buddhist practices into an eminently usable progression of experiential exercises, meditations, observations, and links to audio recordings and other resources. This one book can make one's entire life enterprise more workable. Deep bows."

—Linda Graham, MFT, experienced psychotherapist and author of *Bouncing Back: Rewiring Your Brain for Maximum Resilience and Well-Being*

"Practical, hands-on, and clear, *The Mindfulness-Based Emotional Balance Workbook* lays out a full set of tools for cultivating well-being. Everyone from newcomers to meditation to experienced clinicians and teachers may find something of value here."

—Sharon Salzberg, author of *Lovingkindness* and *Real Happiness*

"Nothing is so taken for granted and yet deserves so much more attention and investigation as our emotions. This very helpful workbook—put together by people who clearly have deeply studied emotion (their own and others')—offers insight and practicality in equal measure. It presents working with emotions not as an arduous struggle but rather as a rich and rewarding journey. Bon voyage!"

—**Barry Boyce,** editor-in-chief of *Mindful* and mi ndful.org

"This remarkable book beautifully integrates key insights of mindfulness and compassion practice toward cultivating greater emotional balance. Guiding us step-by-step, the workbook shows us how to create a more balanced, compassionate, and joyful life. A real gift to the world."

—**Thupten Jinpa,** author of *A Fearless Heart: How the Courage to Be Compassionate Can Transform Our Lives*

"The emotional balance Cullen and Brito Pons write about is not some unattainable calm, but rather the courage of an open heart—one that responds to life with a full range of feelings. Their workbook provides practical and heartful advice for choosing—and changing—your relationship to fear, anger, and resentment, and for cultivating the ability to experience joy, gratitude, and love."

—**Kelly McGonigal, PhD,** author of *The Neuroscience of Change*

"This book is excellent—it's wise and highly practical for emotional clarity and balance. Cullen and Brito Pons have put together a step-by-step prescription for living with greater ease, grace, and happiness."

—**Elisha Goldstein, PhD,** cofounder of The Center for Mindful Living in Los Angeles, CA, and author of *Uncovering Happiness: Overcoming Depression with Mindfulness and Self-Compassion Compassion*

To Sofi and Michael
—M.C.

To my parents, Ana and Iván
—G.B.P.

Foreword

Let's keep one thing squarely in mind as we approach the subject of cultivating greater emotional balance through this wise and engaging workbook—something that it is all too easy to forget. The condition we call "balance" is never static. It is a dynamic process. Take the example of your own body standing. If you look closely and attend to what your muscles are doing and how it actually feels, at a micro level standing "still" actually involves continually *losing* your balance and, somehow, amazingly regaining it, recovering your equilibrium over and over again. It is the same for walking and running. Just watch a toddler moving about: losing balance, recovering it; losing it, recovering it, and learning, learning, learning as she or he engages in endless adventures of discovery, virtually moment by moment.

As adults, it is equally possible for us to live more balanced and therefore more satisfying and effective lives if we are willing to pay attention and learn from those moments when we inevitably lose our balance, as all of us do from time to time, and even in those instances when we literally or metaphorically fall down. That is precisely what the curriculum of this workbook is all about—cultivating the dynamic condition of emotional *balance.* And we could say that that is what the curriculum of life itself is all about as well—if we are willing to embrace our experience in awareness and learn from it, all of it, and so continually grow further and further into our fullness as human beings, just as so magically happens with us when we are young and learning to stand and walk and move about, and yes, to fall and get back up, over and over and over again if necessary. This is part of what the authors refer to as the *miracle* of mindfulness.

The Chinese character for mindfulness consists of the ideogram for *now,* or *presence,* over the ideogram for *heart.* I love that. In Chinese and many other Asian languages, it turns out that the word for "mind" and the word for "heart" are the same word. So if you don't somehow hear or feel the word "heartfulness" as you are reading or hearing "mindfulness," you are not fully grasping the spirit, the meaning, or the invitation of mindfulness as a way of living. I find it insightful and illuminating that the word for "anger" in Chinese also contains the ideogram for "heart." But instead of the ideogram for "now" sitting above it, it has the ideogram for "slave." Pretty telling, isn't it? To me, it suggests that when we are caught up in an emotion like anger, we can all too easily become enslaved. There is nothing wrong with the feeling of anger itself if we can be in wise relationship to it when it arises. Our emotions evolved to help us survive—all of them. But when we are so caught up in anger, or anxiety, or sadness that we literally, as we say, "lose our mind," and with it, lose touch with what might be a healthier and more emotionally intelligent way to be in relationship with what is unfolding, then we are truly imprisoned in that moment, enslaved.

But if we can lose our mind in one moment, we can also recover it in the next moment, just as with our balance.[1] This is very good news—and a door into a process of ongoing learning, growing, healing, and transformation across the lifespan really—with every moment a new beginning, *if* we are willing to open to it as a new and fresh opportunity. And that, again, is precisely the curriculum that this book walks us through, with so much goodwill, care and caring, promise, and respect for your unique history, experience, and aspirations as a reader that you can feel this embrace emanating off the pages as you engage with it.

Mindfulness is ultimately about *relationality* with the full range of our experience, both inwardly and outwardly. So when we are cultivating mindfulness, either through formal meditative practices or informally, in our lives as they are unfolding wherever and whenever we find ourselves, we are literally cultivating intimacy with our own minds, our own hearts, and with our own experience through paying attention to things we might ordinarily never accord any attention to at all. That intimacy is ultimately

---

1 With perhaps a slight delay or refractory period in certain circumstances, which you can also recognize and take into account mindfully, as you will see.

intimacy with your own body, your own mind, your own thoughts and emotions, with others, and with conditions and events in the larger world, and finally with what new ways of being might be possible in this very moment if we can remain awake and aware, or recover quickly if we lose our emotional balance. So it is a very big curriculum, actually the curriculum of life itself while we have the opportunity to be alive. That makes the present moment and how wc are willing to be in relationship to it very very special, right inside its own ordinariness. What better place to place your trust than in your own deepest integrity and beauty, your own innate emotional intelligence, and its cultivability as a skill, as a new way of being and being in relationship to what is and what might emerge?

Then, we can inquire and investigate perhaps a little more deeply into *who* is losing his or her balance? Who is frightened? Who is angry? Who is aware? And is your awareness of your anger angry? It takes an adventurous spirit to investigate in this way and reclaim the full dimensionality of your being. And it also takes trust—in yourself and in those who offer guidance. In this case, with this workbook, you are in very good hands.

I have known Margaret Cullen for a long time. Not only is she a highly experienced MBSR teacher; she has bravely and gladly thrown herself into a wide range of teaching formats, pedagogies, and perspectives over the years, in her aim to integrate the science of emotion with the ever-developing curriculum of mindfulness-based approaches for cultivating greater health and well-being in the broadest, deepest, and wisest lived and embodied expression of those commonly overused terms. And that means developing our health and well-being in the face of the sometimes hugely challenging twists and turns of the human condition, the things and events that can and do happen to us and in us, and to those we know and love, that are difficult, often rending, fear-producing, scary, at times overwhelming, and at times merely disheartening. Margaret's own trajectory to effect this synthesis has not always been easy, but what we benefit from as readers, and as people who will not merely read this book but engage with it as a workbook, is her skill at integrating disparate threads of emotional science, wisdom, and mindfulness meditation practice into one seamless whole. Add to that the background, insights, and contributions of Gonzalo Brito Pons, her coauthor and collaborator, and you have a worthy portal into what is deepest and best, most robust and wisest within yourself, even if you don't believe it at first. That is both the promise and the challenge of authentic mindfulness practice—take it step by step, chapter by chapter, moment by moment, and see what happens. Your life is the laboratory. Why *not* experiment with discovering and strengthening your natural capacity for emotional balance, and with it, the deep satisfaction, sweetness, and equanimity that accompany its embodied expression in the only moment you will ever have—this one?

You could say that we are taking "baby steps" at first, but perhaps we can anticipate what might happen when we take on this opportunity with the same determination and abandon that we naturally brought to moving around when we were learning to stand and to walk and run. You, we, all of us, already are masters of a certain kind of balancing. Let's extend that innate genius of ours into how we live our lives and navigate our emotions, with the careful guidance, support, and wisdom of Margaret and Gonzalo.

—Jon Kabat-Zinn
Cape Cod, Massachusetts
December 28, 2014

Acknowledgments

Every book is an interdependent project that requires the help of many brains, hearts, and hands. We are very grateful for the help and inspiration provided by many people who supported us while writing this book. Although we can't acknowledge in this space everyone who has contributed to this book, we would like to thank at least some of our friends, colleagues, and mentors.

Margaret is especially grateful to:

Jon Kabat-Zinn, who stands in a category by himself for his guidance, encouragement, inspiration, and unstinting generosity.

My teachers: Joseph Goldstein, Jack Kornfield, Sharon Salzberg, Mingyur Rinpoche, Tsoknyi Rinpoche, Pema Chödrön, Yvonne Rand, Shinzen Young, Saki Santorelli, Thupten Jinpa, His Holiness the Dalai Lama, Marshall Rosenberg, Ralph Metzner, Paul Ekman, Georgina Lindsey, and Sofi Cullen.

My colleagues: Linda Wallace, Betsy Hedberg, Erika Rosenberg, Leah Weiss-Ekstrom, Monica Hanson, Kelly McGonigal, Alan Wallace, Amishi Jha, Amy Saltzman, Elana Rosenbaum, Margaret Kemeny, and Robert Roeser. Special thanks to Margaret Stauffer for offering me carte blanche to teach contemplative programs at the Cancer Support Community and to Barbara Gates for launching my writing career.

My benefactors: Ulco Visser, James R. Doty, and Michael Cullen.

My soul sisters: Nancy Rothschild, Pia Stern, Carol Watson, Wendy Zerin, Liz Scott, Catherine Cheyette, and Josephine Coatsworth.

Gonzalo is deeply grateful to:

My teachers: Thich Nhat Hanh, Tsoknyi Rinpoche, Dan Brown, Joe Loizzo, Robert Thurman, Matthieu Ricard, Alan Wallace, Jon Kabat-Zinn, Bob Stahl, Shaila Catherine, Kelly McGonigal, and Rick Hanson.

My colleagues and friends: Catalina Segú, María Noel Anchorena, Santiago Nader, Claudio Araya, Bárbara Porter, Bruno Solari, Guilherme Zavaschi, Ricardo Pulido, Benjamín Zegers, Verónica Guzmán, Álvaro Langer, Fernando de Torrijos, Vicente Simón, María Teresa Miró, Jenny Wade, Scott Johnson, Linda Graham, and Renée Burgard.

We would also like to thank our editors and support staff at New Harbinger for their kindness, patience, and skill. And, last but not least, our students and clients, who have shown us the power, depth, and beauty of the path.

Introduction

The book that you hold in your hands and the program that it contains is part of a tradition of theories and practices that have prompted a silent revolution in the fields of medicine, psychology, and education during the last few decades. This revolution is driven by a fundamental insight that seems to have been overlooked by a Western culture dazzled with the advances of materialist science and technology. The fundamental insight is that consciousness lies at the heart of all human experience, and that the qualities we cultivate in our minds and hearts have a powerful influence on our physical and psychological well-being.

In the gaps where allopathic medicine and mechanistic psychological models have been less successful (from cancer to stress, from chronic pain to recurrent depression, from health prevention to recovery), new integrative paradigms have emerged. These approaches understand the mind and body as interdependent realities and see health as a synthesis of science and art. Some examples include holistic, mind-body, and integrative medicines; positive, integral, systemic, and transpersonal psychologies; and the emerging field of mindfulness-based interventions, to name a few. In all these approaches there's an understanding that the process of healing isn't something that's induced by an external agent; rather, it emerges from an experiential process in which people learn to tap into their own inner capacity to heal and flourish. In this context, human beings are perceived as being far more free and flexible than is believed in deterministic models. Not only does this capacity to learn new ways of perceiving, intending, acting, thinking, and feeling support long-lasting health and happiness, but, as contemporary research has shown, it's even capable of changing our physiology (for example, blood pressure, heart rate, body temperature) and neurology (patterns of neural activation and even brain structures) through experiential education.

The practices offered in this workbook are designed to serve as a guide and companion in your experiential learning process toward emotional balance, a process in which you'll gradually tap into your own inner resources for healing and flourishing. Although the main focus of the practices in this book is emotional healing and establishing new emotional patterns that foster personal and relational well-being, it's clear that emotional health can't be achieved without also addressing other important dimensions, such as thoughts, perceptions, values, intentions, and feelings. This is why we'll spend some time reflecting and working on each of these levels, while keeping in mind the core topic of the book: cultivating sustainable emotional well-being.

Despite the jaw-dropping advancements in technology and the sophistication of modern life, we humans are still challenged by the same old basic themes of life:

searching for meaning; dealing with loss and grief; finding ways to give and receive love and nurturance; working with difficult emotions like fear and anger. In some ways, our present-day hyperconnectivity and fast-paced lifestyle have further exposed our emotional vulnerability, with many of us feeling overwhelmed by the painful experiences of burnout, competitiveness, anxiety, insecurity, and loneliness.

The core theme that we'll explore in depth in this book is the ancient practice of mindfulness, with a particular focus on the healing and prevention of emotional suffering. In this sense, our program draws from, and contributes to, the growing field of mindfulness-based interventions (MBIs). Like many MBIs, this program is inspired by the traditional healing arts and contemplative wisdom of the Buddhist tradition. Most of what we'll be sharing has been learned firsthand, through our own study, reflection, and practice. In this book we won't present mindfulness as a mere cognitive tool, a behavior-changing technique, or the latest stress-reduction method. Although mindfulness can be effective on these levels, reducing its scope to these outcomes can be misleading, and can also prevent us from accessing the full potential of mindfulness practice. Instead, we'll share a view that sees mindfulness as an important element of a wider path that ultimately leads to the unfolding of the deepest human potential for happiness, love, and selfless wisdom. The good news is that the benefits become available from the very first steps you take on this path. In fact, in traditional Buddhist scriptures it's said that the path of mindfulness is "good in the beginning, good in the middle and good in the end" *(Kalama Sutta).*

So many cultures around the world share a history, sometimes forgotten, of honoring the guest, the stranger, and offering him or her the best food in the cupboard or the most comfortable seat in the house. This book is offered to you in this same spirit: please take the very best of what we have learned, with our sincere and heartfelt wish that it might make your journey more comfortable and ease your burden. What you'll find in the pages to come is a weaving together of the fundamentals of mindfulness practice with a variety of ideas, meditative experiments, and off-the-cushion practices that together can transform difficult, and often deeply ingrained, emotional patterns into a path to insight and well-being. As our readers, you are our honored guests, and we invite each of you to come in and make yourself at home in these pages, taking comfort and nourishment from a program that has been honed through many years of experience.

How This Program Evolved

In 2002, I (Margaret) was hired to be the "emotion trainer" in a research study called Cultivating Emotional Balance (CEB). The study was the brainchild of the world-renowned emotion theorist, Paul Ekman, which he developed after he had participated in a "Mind and Life" meeting about Destructive Emotions with His Holiness the Dalai Lama and a group of eminent scholars and practitioners. (This particular meeting has been chronicled in the fascinating book of the same title—*Destructive Emotions*—by meeting participant Dan Goleman.)

As they discussed the different approaches taken in Buddhism and in Western psychology toward the management of challenging emotions, His Holiness suggested that the group combine tools from the East and the West and make them available to a wider audience. With the help of Buddhist scholar, teacher, and translator Alan Wallace, Ekman determined to create a curriculum and offer it to educators, because not only do they experience high degrees of stress, their ability to manage their emotions has a direct impact on the children they teach.

Though Alan and Paul contributed most of the content to CEB, I conceptualized the chronology and organization of the curriculum, as well as the bridging of Buddhist philosophy with Western psychology. In my role as "emotion trainer," I met with Paul weekly to absorb his forty-five years of experience studying emotion and facial expression and developing theories about them. This was no small task for either of us. Paul is nothing if not a demanding teacher, and I came to him already formed, with my own ideas about the nature of emotion that were hard won from countless hours on the meditation cushion.

The project, graced early on with a financial gift from His Holiness, was fraught with challenges. It was ambitious, perhaps overly so, and the science was complex and expensive. There were internal politics and disagreements. Yet in spite of all this, we delivered the ever-evolving intervention to six separate groups of educators in the San Francisco Bay Area, and the results were dramatic. Initial pilot studies and more recent clinical trials have shown that educators who participated in the CEB program decreased depressive and anxious symptoms, reduced negative emotions (such as cynicism and hostility), enhanced positive affect, became better at recognizing facial expressions of emotions and reflecting them, and developed a more flexible and responsive cortisol profile and decreased mental rumination after being exposed to an anxiety-provoking situation. In short, the training helped teachers learn to regain psychological and physiological balance after emotionally upsetting situations. The fact that most of these positive changes were maintained five months after the intervention suggests the long-term benefit of these practices (Kemeny et al. 2012; Turan et al., 2015).

In 2006 Ulco Visser of the Impact Foundation invited me to teach CEB in Denver, Colorado. The results were even more dramatic. Visser was impressed, but he was a businessman at heart and determined to develop a model that could be both scalable and financially self-sustaining. As it stood, with separate instructors for the meditation and psychology components, scalability and sustainability seemed problematic.

So in 2007 Visser made me an offer I couldn't refuse: How would I like to be paid to write "the curriculum of my dreams"? By now I had been involved in many research studies, had become certified as a Mindfulness-Based Stress Reduction (MBSR) teacher, had trained in MBCT (Mindfulness-Based Cognitive Therapy), and MB-Eat (Mindfulness-Based Eating Awareness Training), and had extensive training in group facilitation. What's more, throughout my work on CEB I had often felt that we were reinventing the wheel. So much of what we were trying to accomplish had already been done with MBSR. And yet there was clearly additional value in combining emotion theory with meditation training.

Summary of research outcomes on MBEB with educators

A randomized controlled trial of the MBEB program for parents and teachers of children with special needs found that participants assigned to MBEB showed significant reductions in stress, depression, and anxiety and increased mindfulness, self-compassion, and personal growth at program completion and at two months follow-up, in contrast to wait-list controls. Participants also showed significant positive changes in their relational competence, increasing their capacity for empathic concern and forgiveness. Additionally, MBEB significantly influenced caregiving competence in teachers (Benn, Akiva, Arel, and Roeser 2012).

Two other randomized controlled trials of MBEB examined program effects on Canadian and American public school teachers' mindfulness, occupational self-compassion, stress, and burnout. Teachers randomized to the MBEB program showed greater increases in self-reported mindfulness and self-compassion, greater improvements on a behavioral task requiring focused attention and working memory, and greater reductions in stress and burnout at postprogram and four-month follow-up compared to wait-list controls. Results also showed that postprogram changes in mindfulness and self-compassion mediated reductions in occupational stress, burnout, anxiety, and depression at follow-up (Roeseret al. 2013).

I created a curriculum that reflected what students had demonstrated to be the most helpful to them throughout all of the contemplative interventions I had written and delivered (hundreds at this point). Paul was kind enough to give us permission to use some of the techniques he had created for developing emotional literacy, and I also drew heavily from MBSR. In addition, I had been offering workshops on forgiveness to cancer patients and their families for quite some time and felt strongly that this practice was foundational to emotional balance.

The Mindfulness-Based Emotional Balance program (MBEB) was first piloted in Vancouver to both educators and administrators with great success. This group, and subsequent groups in Boulder, Colorado; Ann Arbor, Michigan; and Berkeley, California, have been studied by Robert Roeser and various colleagues with interesting results (see sidebar). These programs were delivered under the name SMART (Stress Management and Relaxation Training)—a clever acronym, but a name I never liked since it didn't convey anything meaningful about the training. Though the program was offered to educators, it was always designed to be readily and easily translated for any domain: education, health care, parenting, business, sports, etc. In fact, as of this writing, we are offering the second pilot version of MBEB for military spouses, a highly deserving and underserved population, and have recently received funding for a "train the trainer" research project (see sidebar).

A workbook is different from a live class. Writing this book was not simply a matter of adapting our manual (which Linda Wallace and Betsy Hedberg did a superb job of writing) to workbook form. Because there is no teacher and no group to interact with, some components have been removed, and others have been added that lend themselves better to going solo. Also, if there is one thing I have learned from my students again and again, it's that most of us tend to be pretty hard on ourselves. It's easier to strive and tighten than to relax; easier to work than to play. For this reason, we've added "experiments," "exercises," and "field observations" to each of the chapters. These are best approached with a spirit of fun and curiosity.

Finding a balance between effort and relaxation is one of the great arts of living, and it can be understood and refined through mindfulness practice. If you are one of those rare people who are good at playing and bad at working, feel free to skip the experiments! In any case, finding balance is an ongoing challenge because conditions are always changing—in our minds, our bodies, and our circumstances. Learning the art of "right effort," as it's called in Buddhism, will be woven into many of the chapters.

Summary of research outcomes on MBEB with educators

A pilot study carried out by Amishi Jha and her research team at the University of Miami examined MBEB-trained military spouses and compared them to a group of spouses who did not receive training. All fifty spouses in the project completed an intentionally repetitive and monotonous attention task prior to and following the training period, as well as a series of questionnaires about their wellbeing. Preliminary results positively suggest that following the training period, the trained spouses were better able to pay attention and reported lower levels of mind-wandering. These attentional benefits were complemented by higher reported levels of self-compassion and lower levels of perceived stress. Jha has recently received a larger grant from the US Department of Defense to train many more spouses and explore train-the-trainer methods of delivery as well. (Sidebar written by Amishi Jha.)

Who Is Gonzalo and How Did He Become the Coauthor?

Gonzalo is a clinical psychologist, researcher, and contemplative educator. He began his meditation practice in 1999 in the Zen tradition, and the following year he attended a traditional three-month retreat with Venerable Thich Nhat Hanh in Plum Village in southern France, an experience that has inspired his life path and vocation since. Over the years, he has deepened his practice, and since 2005 he has complemented his clinical work with teaching meditation and yoga in clinical, educational, and community settings in Chile, Peru, Argentina, Spain, and the United States.

In 2013 the Center for Compassion and Altruism Research and Education (CCARE) at Stanford offered its first formal instructor-training program. I had the privilege of supervising Gonzalo, who was the first person to be officially "certified" as a Compassion

Cultivation Training instructor. As his supervisor, I was granted intimate access to his meditation practice and consistently found a depth of experience, understanding, and commitment way beyond his years. I also found a fellow traveler who shared many of my perspectives on meditation, compassion, and psychology. In addition to our demanding year-long training at CCARE, Gonzalo was completing a PhD researching the effects of mindfulness-based and compassion-based trainings in psychological and relational well-being, and coauthoring a mindfulness practice book in Spanish. Knowing he had yet to complete his dissertation, I was doubtful he would accept my invitation to cowrite this book, but he did. Writing together has been a great joy, and his contributions have been inestimable.

Who Should Use This Workbook?

Perhaps it would be easier to answer first the question "Who shouldn't use this workbook?" since that category is much smaller. If you are under eighteen years old, we encourage you to explore the many wonderful programs designed for teens and younger age groups. And if you are in crisis, whether physical, emotional, or spiritual, please see an appropriate professional. A workbook can never substitute for a trained and caring "live" ally.

Beyond those two categories, this workbook is appropriate for anyone who is seeking greater emotional balance and ease through the cultivation of mindfulness, kindness, and compassion. It is suitable for those brand-new to mindfulness, as well as those who have some contemplative training.

It's not necessary to feel overwhelmed by emotions to benefit from this program. Whether you would just like to be kinder and less reactive with your family or you suffer from anxiety or low-level depression, this training can help you. Some of you may feel challenged by a recent loss or transition, while others may be seeking a greater sense of integrity or integration. Whatever brings you to these pages, the following are some guidelines that will help you get the most from this workbook.

How to Use This Workbook

The greatest benefits from this program will be derived from your daily practice. Yet it's never easy to make the time for meditation practice, for *so* many reasons: (1) we're all busy; (2) new habits are hard to make and old ones hard to break; (3) we often resist what we *should* be doing; (4) it's harder and harder to simply sit still; (5) we're afraid of facing ourselves and of feeling suppressed emotions; (6) we're deeply conditioned to be "productive"; (7) our households are noisy and distracting ... and the list goes on. Research on MBIs increasingly shows that positive results are dose-related: the more you practice, the greater the benefits.

So, given these challenges, here are some attitudinal foundations that can help you to engage with the practices and get the most out of this workbook. The first seven of these come from Jon Kabat-Zinn's *Full Catastrophe Living* (2013), but then we added a few more for good measure!

1. **Nonjudgment.** This quality of awareness involves cultivating impartial observation in regard to any experience—not labeling thoughts, feelings, or sensations as good or bad, right or wrong, fair or unfair, but simply taking note of thoughts, feelings, or sensations in each moment.

2. **Patience.** This is an expression of wisdom and maturity. It acknowledges that things must unfold in their own time and is a wonderful antidote to the agitation that can escalate around resisting the truth of the present moment.

3. **Beginner's Mind.** This quality of awareness sees things as new and fresh, as if for the first time, with a sense of curiosity.

4. **Trust.** This is about honoring your own experience and learning how to listen deeply to your own heart, mind, and body. There will be times throughout the course of this training, and certainly in life, when your inner experience is in conflict with what is being asked of you. Learning how to trust yourself is essential to engaging with these practices and cultivating emotional balance.

5. **Nonstriving.** With this quality of awareness, there is no grasping, aversion to change, or movement away from whatever arises in the moment; in other words, nonstriving means not trying to get anywhere other than where you are.

6. **Acceptance.** This quality of awareness validates and acknowledges things as they are. To accept the truth doesn't necessarily mean you have to love it, or even like it. It is really about connecting with what is true in each moment and fighting the tendency to deny, reject, or avoid.

7. **Letting Be.** Although Kabat-Zinn uses the phrase "Letting Go," we prefer to soften this a little. For many people, letting go is a slippery slope on the way to actively pushing away what is unwanted. With this quality of awareness, you can simply let things be as they are, with no need to try to let GO of whatever is present.

8. **Humor.** Although humor can't be forced, it can be welcomed and encouraged. And humor is a great ally when it comes to watching the machinations of your own mind. Like many of the attitudes on this list, humor creates space in the mind and counteracts the tendencies to tighten and contract in response to unpleasant experience.

9. **Curiosity.** Many of the insights that lead to emotional balance involve seeing things as they are while at the same time inquiring into their causality and consequences.

10. **Affection.** Kabat-Zinn sometimes describes mindfulness as "affectionate attention." When awareness is imbued with the qualities of warmth and tenderness, it's much easier to move in close to experience and to know it fully, especially when that experience is painful or invokes feelings of vulnerability.

We encourage you to approach these qualities or attitudes as touchstones, rather than as mandates. None of us will ever fully embody these qualities in every moment. And even meditation and compassion cultivation can become co-opted by past conditioning into yet another way to beat ourselves up.

Part 1

Foundations

Chapter 1

Mindfulness

THE KEY TO EMOTIONAL BALANCE

Something led you to pick up this particular book. Perhaps you've had some exposure to mindfulness. Maybe you've read about research studies showing the many benefits of mindfulness, or maybe you have some friends who took a class and they seem happier and kinder, or report that they're sleeping better and have more energy. Maybe you were charmed by the wide gamut of people singing the praises of mindfulness, from Congressman Tim Ryan to the famous basketball coach Phil Jackson. Or maybe something deep inside just knows that the answer you are looking for is locked inside you, and mindfulness has the key.

You may also have found your way to this particular book because the challenges of life have, at times, felt overwhelming; because the all-too-human emotions that have helped you to survive have also felt somehow threatening or problematic. It may be that your nervous system is feeling taxed or depleted, unable to bear the intensity of what rises up within. Or it may be that there's one particular emotion you find challenging, such as anger or fear.

Whatever led you here, we are deeply respectful of the path that has brought you to our "doorstep" of this first chapter, because we know, from our own personal and sometimes painful experiences, that the road has not been easy, pleasant, or straight; that the journey to this particular juncture has been fraught with perils (both real and imagined); that the travel has been arduous and taxing, yet somehow you have continued to put one foot in front of the other; and that along the way you've known great joy and satisfaction as well as deep sorrow and disappointment. We also recognize that something about mindfulness has called your attention; that deep down, when you tap into your inner wellspring of resources and wisdom, there's an intuition that mindfulness practice could resonate with you in a way that nothing else has.

Our deepest intention for this book is that through it, and the program described in its pages, you'll find a way to connect with this deep inner knowing and to tap into the potential of mindfulness to transform difficult emotions, troubling thoughts, and painful sensations. All this, through the extraordinarily simple and yet incredibly challenging practice of mindfulness in daily life, moment by moment.

Welcome to the present moment. Like the sign at the casino says, "You must be present to win."

The Essence of the Miracle

Perhaps the most widely cited definition of mindfulness is the one put forth in 2005 by Jon Kabat-Zinn, creator of Mindfulness-Based Stress Reduction (MBSR) and generally considered the "father" of mindfulness in the West: "moment-to-moment, non-judgmental awareness, cultivated by paying attention in a specific way, that is, in the present moment, and as nonreactively, as non-judgmentally, and openheartedly as possible" (Kabat-Zinn 2005, 108).

While at first glance this might feel like a tall order, let's begin to unpack this notion—which is translated as mindfulness from the original Sanskrit word *sati*—and, in keeping with Kabat-Zinn's approach, explore what it really means as a way of living life and working with all the richness and complexity of our lives as they actually are. Taking each component of this definition in turn, let's see what we can glean, while simultaneously appreciating that anything, especially a notion like mindfulness, is so much more than the reassembled sum of its component parts. Let's begin with the parts and see where they lead.

"...moment-to-moment..."

As clichéd as it may sound, we truly only have moments to live. Despite all our scheming and planning for the future, all our reminiscing and recalling of the past, and all the dreaming of other imagined possibilities that our wonderfully creative human minds can accomplish, this moment is the only place we can be.

And yet we each have this amazing and complicated human brain, capable of so much more than "just" present-moment awareness. It can plan, anticipate, remember, construct stories and scenarios, develop scripts and patterns of behavior that reside below our day-to-day awareness, and generally get us into more imagined mischief in an hour than we can *actually* get into in a lifetime! *If* we let it. And therein lies the key to mindfulness: noticing when we're not actually in the present moment and bringing ourselves back.

"...awareness..."

So, if noticing is crucial to mindfulness, then it follows that awareness must figure into the equation. What *is* noticing, really, if not the product of awareness? We shine the floodlight of attention on our experience, moment to moment, and sometimes (frequently) we notice things. All sorts of experiences arise within the field of awareness: an itchy nose (bodily sensation), a notion about what you would like for breakfast (thought), a deep longing for another person (emotion), and a plethora of other experiences in any given moment. Awareness is the capacity to witness and hold all these various events as they appear. To use a traditional simile, awareness is like the vast sky in which clouds of all different shapes (our experiences) appear and disappear. The sky isn't the clouds and it's not affected by the clouds, just like experiences (an itch, a smell, a thought, or an emotion) can appear in the space of awareness without affecting awareness. If it sounds obscure at this point, don't worry—we'll explore this point in more depth soon, and there will be plenty of opportunities in this book and in the accompanying guided meditations to explore it experientially. For now, simply consider the idea that we are always *in a relationship with* the experiences that appear in our field of awareness and, just like any relationship, things can get complicated. In a nutshell, mindfulness practice involves cultivating a healthy relationship with our experience, a relationship characterized by presence and acceptance.

Most of us are comfortable with the process of considering our relationships with other human beings, but rarely do we remember that we also have relationships with the things that arise within our own bodies, minds, and hearts. If you doubt this, try a little thought experiment: Call to mind a place that holds great meaning for you. Picture that place in your mind and perhaps invite in a recollection of its sights, sounds, smells, and tastes. Notice what arises around the simple recollection of this place. Is there warmth, longing, perhaps even aversion or strong negative emotion for some reason? You may find yourself wanting to linger on the idea of this place, to savor this sense of it in this moment, or you may want to push away that image because it's too painful or provocative just now.

In the space between a mental phenomenon (the arising of an image or idea of this meaningful place) and the fullness of what you actually noticed around the phenomena lies your relationship with it. A desire to move in closer or pull it toward you, an aversion that impels you to move away or escape it, maybe even a kind of denial or pretending it isn't present. Such aversions, desires, and delusions are at the heart of suffering, and these relationships are what we're pointing to.

"...by paying attention in a specific way, that is, in the present moment, and as non-reactively, as non-judgmentally..."

When using the phrase "non-judgmentally" Kabat-Zinn is pointing our attention toward *how we relate* to our moment-to-moment experience, instead of toward *the objects* of that awareness. He's inviting us to meet each arising experience with a willingness to see it in its fullness, without becoming entangled, enmeshed, or identified with it in any way. He's also asking us to let go of evaluating sensations, thoughts, or emotions as inherently good or bad; instead, we note their presence and allow them to be here because they *already are* present. And yet, how often have you noticed an inner commentary that says something like "I shouldn't be thinking that," or "See! This is the problem with me and how I _____ (fill in the blank)." Can you entertain the possibility that these thoughts, too, can be seen as further brain secretions that can also be noticed, rather than believed and acted upon? This is the nonjudgment to which we are referring.

It's worth noting that nonjudgment doesn't mean giving up your capacity to *discern*—the ability to recognize the relative merits or possibilities in choices and to make those choices on a consistent basis. Sometimes when people hear "nonjudgmental" they imagine passivity so extreme it verges on inertia, where everything is viewed as allowable and every situation is met with a "go with the flow" attitude. Nothing could be further from the truth. We're cultivating this very fine-tuned awareness of what is arising and, in the light of this abiding awareness, we're able to untangle the reality of what is occurring from our own reactions to that reality (thoughts, feelings, memories, old habits, old wounds) and from there to *discern* and decide on a skillful and nonreactive response that draws from a deep inner wisdom of what is appropriate. Sometimes that wise response involves strong action, sometimes it calls for measured action, and still other times, the skillful choice may be no action at all. (Throughout the book, we use the word "skillful" to mean well-advised, wholesome, and effective, rather than the more common usage suggesting competence or proficiency at a sport or musical instrument, for example.) The key is that we're now captains of our own ship, so to speak, and not servants of our conditioned reactions.

Let's take the example of cheesecake. A scrumptious and pleasing example if ever there was one! And let's say that you're watching your diet because you've been warned that you're edging toward type 2 diabetes. This strawberry delight with deep dark chocolate drizzled on top does not lie on your personal path to freedom from diabetes, by any means. And yet, when you find this piece of cheesecake sitting before you, the pull toward savoring and devouring it is almost irresistible. Almost. Perhaps in the past you've noticed yourself thinking (or even saying), "Oh no, I couldn't!" and then, seemingly seconds later, found yourself contemplating a few crumbs on your plate and a very full feeling in your belly. Not to mention a vague (or not so vague) feeling of guilt and shame over having consumed the cheesecake when you knew at some deeper level that you shouldn't have.

Mindfulness in this situation could allow you to hold in awareness the cheesecake itself, and all that comes up in your mind and heart and body *around* that cheesecake (both for and against consumption!), and to then *choose* among the various options available to you the one that is most in service of what matters to you in the bigger picture. This is the value of discernment.

"...and openheartedly as possible."

And so we arrive at the attitude of mindfulness. Inherent in this present-moment willingness to encounter all that arises, nonreactively and without judgment, is a stance of patience, kindness, and friendliness. One way to describe how we meet each moment and each experience is with a kind of gentle curiosity that might even have an undercurrent of playfulness or lightheartedness. People often mistake the attitude of mindfulness for one of rigid resolve and stern intention. Jack Kornfield (2012) calls on his own decades of meditation practice to describe this common mistake:

> I used to think that to become free you had to practice like a samurai warrior, but now I understand that you have to practice like a devoted mother of a newborn child. It takes the same energy but has a completely different quality. It's unwavering compassion and presence

that liberates rather than having to defeat the enemy in battle.

Practicing like a samurai warrior may even elicit a kind of resistance to experience that's not consistent with mindfulness practice. Instead, we're invited to soften our stance (perhaps both physically and attitudinally) and be willing to move in closer to the phenomena arising with curiosity and kind willingness. The intention is to be fully in contact with the experience and *know* it in a way that allows us to then respond in new and potentially fruitful ways.

This openhearted curiosity can be likened to the way ancient explorers related to the physical world. What comes to mind are those ancient maps that included details about places where some intrepid souls had ventured forth and taken the time to describe their discoveries. And then out on the edges of the map, where nobody had yet traveled, were admonitions to everyone else that read "Beyond, there be dragons!" These dire warnings were not, of course, placed there because people had encountered fire-breathing serpents in that particular region and returned with singed sails and bite marks on their hulls, but as indicators that this was unknown territory that one should enter only at one's own peril.

But those intrepid explorers who came after were willing to sail out and cautiously explore these unknown seas, circumspect but curious. They opened up to the possibility of all that might arise, and they kept to their intended journeys nonetheless, calmly preparing to be unprepared, and full of hope and possibility for what might be encountered. Openheartedness ultimately led to discovery, understanding, wisdom, and learning, and no dragons were harmed in the creation of this new world. A fruitful outcome indeed!

Exercise: Recognizing Mindful Moments

Keeping in mind the definition of mindfulness we've been exploring so far (namely, moment-to-moment, nonjudgmental awareness, cultivated by paying attention in the present moment as nonreactively, nonjudgmentally, and openheartedly as possible), remember a moment in your life in which mindfulness was present. It could have been a moment in solitude, or a situation with someone else in which you offered or received the quality of mindful presence. What was happening? How did mindfulness affect the situation? How did you feel? Why do you think this experience has stayed in your memory? Take a moment to write down your answers in the space provided.

Notes

_____

Now, take a few deep breaths and stretch your body gently, let go of the memory you just evoked, and bring your attention fully to the present moment, embodying the qualities of mindfulness we explored earlier. Take this invitation as playfully as possible: Can you attend to your own experience with a fresh perspective, suspending habitual judgments, as if you were noticing things for the first time?

What do you notice right now? You can simply pay attention to whatever enters your field of awareness (sights, sounds, smells, textures, thoughts, emotions, and so on) or you can take a few minutes to notice specific aspects of your present-moment experience. For example, the sensations of the contact of your body with the chair and the floor; the sounds that you hear; or the colors and shapes in your visual field. Again, use the space below to write down your observations.

Notes

_____

And so we've unpacked a widely accepted definition of mindfulness and explored each component in some depth, while also seeing each component as part of a larger whole. But somehow this reassembled whole does not fully capture the profoundly transformative power of mindfulness. The miracle of mindfulness is still left to explore.

> Mindfulness is the miracle by which we master and restore ourselves. It is the miracle which can call back in a flash our dispersed mind and restore it to wholeness so that we can live each minute

of life. Consider for example a magician who cuts his body into many parts and places each part in a different region—hands in the south, arms in the east, legs in the north, and then by some miraculous power lets forth a cry which reassembles every part of his body. Mindfulness is like that! (Nhat Hanh 1987, 14)

The miracle of mindfulness is this possibility of reassembling and restoring the sense of wholeness and presence that has become elusive for so many of us. In the hurry of modern life, where multitasking and 24/7 connectivity have become part of the usual landscape, it's not uncommon to be running constantly to meet the demands of a busy life. This makes it natural, and even at times adaptive, to default into *reacting* instead of *responding* to circumstances. Although mindfulness has always been "miraculous," the renewed interest in these practices may have something to do with how increasingly scattered we've become. Our emotional lives are especially sensitive to, and intimately connected with, how mindful (or unmindful) we are. When we're scattered and live mostly on "autopilot," we're more likely to become overwhelmed by strong emotions and to habitually repeat deeply rooted patterns of emotional reactivity. Without the spaciousness of mindful awareness, we become slaves to our own patterns.

Here's a real-life story of the miraculous power of mindfulness in the face of difficult emotions. It took place during a winter retreat at Plum Village, the main retreat center of Vietnamese Buddhist teacher Thich Nhat Hanh, in southern France. As part of the daily routine in this meditation center, there were several reminders for cultivating mindfulness in the midst of daily activities, helping everyone to slowly transform the habit patterns of mindlessness and reactivity. Two of those devices were the sound of a bell that rang every half hour and the telephone ringing in the dining hall. Upon hearing either sound, everyone would stop what they were doing, stand or sit upright, breathe deeply three times, relax their faces, and, with a half-smile on their lips, silently enjoy their breathing or recite the following *gatha,* or verse, in their minds: "Listen, listen. This wonderful sound brings me back to my true home."

One of the retreatants that winter was a young French fellow in his late teens who was suffering from chronic depression, and just by looking at his expression you could guess that his mind was stuck in negative rumination and self-judgment much of the time. But every time he heard the bell or telephone, he found a way out of his mental prison: he opened his chest, straightened his spine, gently smiled, and breathed deeply. Sometimes he would tell you, with a relieved expression on his face: *"Ce téléphone m'a sauvé la vie"* ("This telephone has saved my life"). The sight of his young face relaxing, his intense frown melting, and his body opening through mindful breathing was simple yet powerful evidence that there exists an opportunity for all of us to break the cycle of reactivity and step into freedom.

There's no single greater source of inspiration for our own respective meditation practices than our students. For many years, we've taught mindfulness programs to hundreds of people from all walks of life, ranging in age from 18 to 88, from vibrant health to the last stages of dying, with diagnoses ranging from mild depression to bipolar disorder and a wide range of physical ailments. The miracle of mindfulness has been to see, again and again, that your wholeness can be reclaimed *no matter what* your circumstances are. Irrespective of our diagnosis or circumstances, it's possible for each one of us to access that dimension of our being that is capable of finding freedom and peace in the present moment. When this happens, particularly amidst the turmoil of emotional or physical distress, it feels like a miracle. This is not to say that mindfulness is a substitute for medical or psychological treatment. It is not! In fact, mindfulness often cultivates the discernment necessary to take appropriate action and get the help that's needed. Meditation is not a substitute for medical or psychological treatment, and everyone's needs are different, both from person to person and across an individual's span of development. In fact, most meditation teachers will readily admit to seeking psychological help in the form of therapy or pharmaceuticals at different stages of their lives.

Chapter 2

Emotions

WHAT DRIVE US, AND WHAT
DRIVE US ASTRAY

The mindful way to emotional balance involves contacting and living our emotions fully, and at the same time patiently cultivating the habits of the heart and mind that will foster peace and joy in us and in those around us. Vietnamese Buddhist teacher Thich Nhat Hanh often likens the process of cultivating the mind-heart to the work of an organic gardener. A good gardener acquires, through patient observation and practice, the wisdom and the tools necessary to aid in the process of transforming wholesome seeds into beautiful plants. She also slowly learns how to keep weeds at bay—not by poisoning them, but simply by not feeding them. And she even learns to transform garbage into beautiful flowers. But first, the gardener has to become familiar with the seeds and the land so that she knows exactly how much water is required, how much compost is needed, and which plants grow together well.

Before we start working in our own garden, we too have to become familiar with the nature, function, and dynamics of the emotional seeds within us. By looking deeply at how emotions work, we can realize how related they are to the reality we perceive and inhabit, and how much freedom we actually have to change ingrained emotional habits.

Emotions Are Confusing and Scary!

"Emotion"—it's not an esoteric word, one that conjures up visions of dictionaries or Wikipedia. It seems relatively straightforward and common. When recounting an emotional episode, it's reasonable to expect that there is a shared understanding of what it means. And yet, the more you read about emotions, the more confusing they become.

As with many everyday experiences, scientists don't agree on what emotions actually are. What's worse, emotions are relevant to several domains of study, such as philosophy, psychology, sociology, and even economics, and *they* don't agree either as to what comprises an emotion. On top of this, there are cultural differences with regard to the language and physical expressions of emotion that further confound the issue. For starters, there *is* no word for "emotion" in Tibetan, Tahitian, or Samoan. The Yorubas lack a word for anxiety, and the Tahitians lack a word for sadness. English doesn't have a single-word equivalent for the German *schadenfreude* (pleasure derived from the misfortune of another) or the Japanese *amae* (pleasant feeling of dependence on someone).

The idea that emotions are threatening has a long history. Judeo-Christian societies carry the unconscious imprint of the notion that humans were expelled from the Garden of Eden due to our forebears' yielding to temptation, the *original sin* that's transmitted from generation to generation. Self-flagellation is still used in various religions and cultures to tame the "poor brother ass"—as St. Francis of Assisi called his body—which was believed to be the seat of instincts, desires, and emotions that can lead us astray from virtue. Philosophers, dating back at least to Socrates, have asserted that emotions needed to be controlled by reason, and Sigmund Freud, the father of psychoanalysis, proposed that the immediate gratification of desires (the pleasure principle) had to become educated and civilized (the reality principle).

For many of us, this idea was abundantly reinforced by families and societies that urged us not to express emotions such as desire, sadness, fear, or anger. ("Stop crying or I'll give you something to cry about!") This is one reason why emotions are often experienced as a "black box"—opaque, inscrutable, unpredictable, and potentially dangerous. It's not uncommon to say to someone, "Gee, you look angry," and have him shout back, "I'm not angry! I'm fine!" Or to ask someone how he's feeling and see him puzzled, as if you had asked him to compute the square root of pi.

In this chapter, we'll talk about how emotions work and how we can relate to them more mindfully, exploring ways to regulate them that move beyond repression, suppression, or blind expression. Mindfulness practice offers a very specific toolkit for cultivating and sustaining awareness of all mental, emotional, and physical states. When combined with some intellectual understanding, emotion regulation and balance become attainable, moment by changing moment. The mindful way to emotional balance that we'll explore in this book involves contacting and accepting our emotions fully and at the same time cultivating the habits of the heart and mind that will foster peace and joy in us and in those around us.

Emotion theory provides a map for the often uncharted territory of the affective domain, and it normalizes private inner worlds that can often feel crazy and frightening when kept in the "black box" of denial and repression. The students in our classes have shown us time and time again that understanding certain key concepts about emotions helped them to bring mindful awareness to these feelings when they arose, whether during meditation or in everyday life. It was an unbeatable combination, and it is the premise of this book. Rather than present the latest or purportedly most scientific information, we'd like to share with you what has helped the people we've worked with over many years.

What Are Emotions?

Emotion is a process, a particular kind of automatic appraisal influenced by our evolutionary and personal past, in which we sense that something important to our welfare is occurring, and a set of physiological changes and emotional behaviors begins to deal with the situation. (Ekman 2003, 13)

Most of the ideas in this part of the book come from the groundbreaking work of Paul Ekman, emeritus professor of psychology at the University of California at San Francisco, who looks to evolutionary theory for a good deal of his research and ideas on the meaning and function of emotion. Emotions evolved as a part of our survival mechanisms. This process, which Ekman calls "automatic appraising," became hardwired in us, allowing us to flee or freeze when afraid, to remove obstacles when angry, and to elicit comfort when sad. That's why it's really hard to change what we become emotional about. Emotions were designed to happen without thinking—to move us to action and to safety without stopping to analyze. So these "automatic appraisers" are constantly scanning our experience to see if there's a lurking threat to our welfare or an opportunity that we can take advantage of. When they react, it's without our consent, and often without our awareness. Understanding this has been a huge relief to the students in our classes. It's captured perfectly in Wes Nisker's wonderful quote, "You are not your fault" (2008, 140). What a relief to take yourself off the hook!

Think about this for a second. You've been endowed with a nervous system that has evolved over thousands of generations in a way that you didn't choose. By the time you actually realize that you have a mind and a brain, the basic rules of how they work are already in place. The events that trigger these auto-appraisers are sometimes universal and sometimes personal. Almost anyone would feel fear at the sight of an oncoming car, but while some of us are afraid of hiking down steep trails, others happily scramble down them like mountain goats. Some people have fears of spiders (arachnophobia), heights (acrophobia), and even buttons (koumpounophobia). These personal triggers often come from early childhood and can be carried quite unconsciously into adulthood. Much of psychotherapy is geared toward exploring these "imported scripts" from the past. It can be very helpful to begin to understand your own imported scripts, and we'll explore this later in the book.

There are other ways that emotions can be triggered besides the auto-appraisers. Remembering, talking about, or imagining a past emotional scene or thinking of future scenarios can trigger emotions. Observing another person's emotions (even on a TV screen) can elicit an emotional response. Emotions can be evoked through instruction and also through the voluntary enactment of emotional events, such as in role-play or theater. We can also become emotional by witnessing or becoming aware of norm violations (like talking on a cell phone at the symphony or throwing trash into the street).

Regardless of the kind of trigger, emotional responses can be either functional or dysfunctional. If we automatically swerve away from an oncoming car, the fear response is extremely functional. If we're afraid to leave the house for fear something terrible will happen, we are now in a disorder that is on the very dysfunctional side of fear, a disorder that most likely is being triggered by an imported script from past trauma. If such imported scripts are closely connected to the universal themes, they naturally tend to be more deeply rooted and harder to change. The universal theme for sadness is loss; for anger, thwarted goals; for fear, physical or other harm.

An insight that can bring relief in difficult situations and that also happens to be true when it comes to emotion is "This, too, shall pass." Emotions tend to be quick, and in spite of individual differences, they are distinguished from other aspects of emotional life by their tendency to rapidly arise and pass away. While emotions may last from seconds to minutes, moods can last hours or days. Longer still are traits, which may persist throughout the lifespan. Both moods and traits increase our propensity to experience related emotions. For example, when you're feeling irritable, you're more likely to have moments of anger. If you have a melancholic temperament, you'll experience more moments of sadness.

Emotions are fundamental to the experience of sentient beings. Close your eyes for a moment and just imagine how life would be without them. Most probably, although emotions can sometimes feel overwhelming, the prospect of living a life without emotions will seem dull and boring. In fact, we need emotions to guide our actions, to make sense of our circumstances, to organize our priorities, and to focus our energies in meaningful directions. This is suggested by the word itself, which comes from the Latin *emovere*—from *e-*(out) and *movere* (move)—*emotions set us in motion.*

Emotions Create Realities

To make sense of the way our emotions help us move in the world, the British clinical psychologist and emotion researcher Paul Gilbert has proposed that humans have three main *emotion-regulation systems,* which are sets of basic emotional functions that emerged in our evolutionary history to provide individuals with relevant moment-to-moment information about their environment, and to set in motion specific motivational strategies. These systems are the threat and protection system; the drive, resource-seeking, and excitement system; and the contentment, soothing, and safeness system (Gilbert 2009). Let's take a brief look at these three emotion-regulation systems to better understand how emotions work and how they've evolved to secure our survival.

The *threat system* is directed toward noticing potential risks in the environment, and it produces bursts of feelings such as anxiety, anger, or disgust. This system is responsible for mobilizing fast action to ensure survival. The arousal associated with these feelings in the body creates the necessary alertness that prepares you to act promptly. For example, when a car speeds toward you or someone throws a heavy object at you, it's the threat system that allows you to react effectively to avoid the imminent threat, instead of having to think or plan an action. This is the system that tells you, *You're in trouble: run, fight, or pretend you're dead*—a function that overlaps with Ekman's idea of auto-appraisers.

The *drive system* regulates emotions and motivations related to seeking important resources in the environment, including food, sexual opportunities, alliances, nest sites, and territories. It is a system of desires that moves humans toward important goals and rewards through hyperarousal and positive feelings such as excitement and pleasure. This system moves us to seek satisfaction of material and immaterial wants and needs, including those linked with maintaining self-esteem, such as status-seeking and competitiveness. This system is activated when you're about to get a promotion at work or when you go out for a first date with someone you really like. This is the system that tells you: *What are you waiting for? Just go and get it! It isn't gonna be there forever.*

Finally, the *soothing or calming system* is related to the emotional qualities of contentment and social safety, which involve not only the absence of threat, but also calm and pleasant emotions and a sense of well-being. This system is activated when we spend time with people with whom we feel emotionally connected, attuned, and safe, particularly friends and family members. Interestingly, this system is also activated when we do mindfulness practices and heart practices, such as loving-kindness and compassion meditations (see chapters 9 and 11). This implies that building positive and secure relationships with others and with ourselves makes us feel safe and content. Activating this system tends to downregulate the threat protection and drive systems. This is the system that tells you: *Relax, enjoy, and connect. Everything's fine.*

From childhood on, particularly when the relationship between child and caretaker is healthy, humans (and actually all mammals) learn that safety and contentment are accessible through the activation of the soothing system, which can regulate anxiety, fear, and anger. When this happens, oxytocin, the wonderful neuro-hormone of bonding and connection, elicits in the body and mind feelings of trust, of affiliation, and of being soothed in relationships. Oxytocin also reduces sensitivity to threats in the fear circuits of the *amygdala*—the brain's small but powerful danger alarm.

Until around the 1970s, it was commonly believed that the nervous system was essentially fixed throughout adulthood; that brain functions remained constant and that it was impossible for new neurons to develop after birth. If you were born with a "glass half-empty" attitude, it would be a life sentence of unhappiness. Neuroscience has changed all that with the concept of neuroplasticity, which suggests that, in reality, human brains are flexible and change through experience. This means that although there are some fixed rules about what minds and brains can do (which is why "you are not your fault"), it's also true that we're not biologically or psychologically determined, and that there's an actual space of freedom to respond rather than react that can be cultivated through mindful observation and practice.

Consciously or not, we're constantly training our minds and brains to respond to circumstances in different ways. By virtue of repetition, our reactions crystallize into emotional patterns and neural pathways, which, in turn, influence the way we perceive reality. This is particularly true when we're in the grip of a strong emotion, which is sometimes called the *refractory period* (Ekman 2003), a period of time when we're only able to take in information and evoke memories that confirm, maintain, or justify the emotion we are feeling. This same mechanism that guides and focuses our attention can also limit our capacity to both take in new information and access knowledge already stored that does not match the current emotion. We can all think of countless examples when we have missed obvious cues or forgotten historical data when we were "blinded" by a strong emotion. As Abraham

Maslow (1966, 15) succinctly put it, "I suppose it is tempting, if the only tool you have is a hammer, to treat everything as if it were a nail."

Our invitation in this book is to explore different observational, meditative, and reflective tools that can slowly infuse your emotional life with the warm spaciousness of mindful awareness. As we'll begin to explore soon, moment by moment you have in your hands a gap of freedom in which to gradually cultivate a way of relating to your experiences—including your emotions—that can bring a quality of spaciousness and openness to whatever you're experiencing. This doesn't mean that difficult emotions will magically disappear. Pleasant and unpleasant emotions are just facts of life, and we are not here to cut ourselves off from any aspect of life. The miracle of mindfulness consists precisely of learning to accept experience rather than to fight it, and it's this openhearted acceptance that actually allows change to take place.

Based on his unshakeable faith in basic human goodness, Tibetan meditation teacher Chögyam Trungpa was fond of saying that no matter where you are, your situation is *workable:* "Everything that goes on in our life situation, all the types of emotion, is workable. The inherent essence of situations is workable, and the apparent qualities of situations are workable as well" (Trungpa 2003, 512). That *workability* of your situation is the space between stimulus and response that we'll explore in the following chapter, and it's the field in which we'll cultivate the seeds of emotional balance through the exercises and practices in part 2.

Chapter 3

Clarifying Values and Intentions

WHY ARE YOU HERE?

What are intentions and values, and what do they have to do with emotional balance? Intentions are the thoughts or impulses that drive behavior, and values are the expressions of what you really care about. Even when you're not fully aware of the intentions that drive your behavior, they remain as the invisible but operative force that defines the quality of what you think, say, and do. As Sharon Salzberg (2004) wrote: "Each decision we make, each action we take, is born out of an intention."

One powerful way to strengthen emotional balance is to clarify your intentions and reconnect with your deepest values. In fact, *emotional balance* is intimately related to *cognitive balance* (a healthy way of thinking and knowing), and *conative* or *intentional balance* (a healthy way of relating to intentions). Taken together, cognition, emotion, and intention are three basic aspects of the mind. While cognition deals with the "what" of the mind—knowledge and information—and emotion refers to "how" we feel about this knowledge, intention is the "why." It's how humans translate what they feel about what they know into what they do. Intentions also give meaning and direction to the way we think, feel, and act in the world.

And why choose to do anything, unless it enhances meaning in your life? Before you embark on the practices offered in part 2 of this book, we invite you to stop and consider what your intentions and aspirations are, and how these connect with your deepest values. Values and intentions are like the rudder that guides the boat. On the rough seas of strong emotions, having a sturdy rudder allows the boat to stay the course. And when an action is connected with a conscious intention that is rooted in your core values, not only will this help you achieve your chosen outcome, it can be a touchstone to return to when resistance inevitably arises.

What Are Intentions?

Intention can be understood as the invisible force that precedes all behavior. Though often unconscious, it's a thought, decision, or impulse that impels the body to move in some way. Before you raise your arm, there's an intention to do so; before you scratch an itch, there's an intention to do so; and so on. In fact, before any action, no matter how seemingly trivial and insignificant, there's an intention that precedes it.

Rarely are we asked to pay attention to our intentions *as they are happening,* yet it's quite possible to do so. Let's explore this with a short experiment.

Experiment: Noticing Intention

As you read these words, at some point you'll want to move your body to relieve a feeling of restlessness or discomfort. See if you can catch the feeling of discomfort before you actually move, and delay the response by thirty seconds or so. In that short amount of time, you can sense the intention to move, that "about to" moment in which the body is leaning into the next action. If you can feel this, you have "caught" the moment of intention preceding the action.

This simple exercise might seem trivial at first glance, but it actually opens the door to a deeper truth. The moment of intention before you scratch your nose is an example of a benign and seemingly unimportant intention. But life is made up of these simple moments, and if we're constantly moving from one action to the next, unaware of our intentions, it's quite possible to end up living our whole life on autopilot. This has consequences on many levels. Emotional dysregulation is often a function of several discrete moments of cause and effect that happen so quickly they are below the threshold of conscious awareness. Tuning in to intention is one way to short-circuit the snowball effect that may result in unintended behavior.

For example, let's say you find yourself yelling at a family member and you have no idea why. You might even find yourself in that classic situation of insisting you're not mad as you storm out of the room and slam the door. If you looked closely, you could probably trace back through a series of tiny "mind moments" that would reveal a logical process of cause and effect. It might look something like this: A superior at work made a comment in passing about your performance that raised a kernel of doubt in your mind about your future in that job; that "mental state" of doubt caused you to misinterpret (through personalizing) a memo that was sent to the whole staff. You can see where this is going. As soon as you get home, your partner tells you about various things that need fixing at home. They all involve expenditures. You blow up, not even realizing that, in the back of your mind, you're worried about your job. Even if you miss the moment of distress when your boss tosses out the comment that upset you, it's possible to notice—and even *choose*—your intention before you walk into the house after work. Some physicians in our courses report that they use the simple moment of reaching out to open the door of the exam room to check in on their intention before greeting each new patient.

In our clinical work, it's not uncommon to hear people say they feel as if they've lived for decades without knowing what was really going with them: drifting along in their lives, working in jobs that didn't reflect their values, maintaining relationships that weren't satisfying, or buying things they didn't really want or need. It's as if they were driven by someone else's intentions in a sort of hypnotic trance. The poignancy of this is captured beautifully in the following line from an anonymous AT&T executive: "Ten years ago I turned my face for a moment and it became my life" (Whyte 2002, 231).

Why Notice Intentions?

If you were able to notice an itch and delay scratching it, this is actually quite a powerful practice. Why? First of all, you learn that you can tolerate the discomfort of the itch without needing to scratch immediately. Itches are a great metaphor for all the discomforts that present themselves as urgent, requiring an immediate response. Without awareness of this "about to" moment, we simply scratch, mindlessly attempting to relieve the discomfort of the itch. Have you ever noticed that scratching is often an ineffectual way to relieve the discomfort of itching? The discomfort stops for a moment, but often comes back even stronger. If you can ride out the discomfort of the itch without scratching, it goes away eventually. Each time you delay or forgo the mindless reactions to minor discomforts, you increase your ability to refrain from the compulsive need to avoid unpleasantness, and strengthen the muscles of restraint and willpower.

Another important outcome of noticing intention is the increased possibility for choice. It's difficult to exert free will as your hand goes into the freezer, takes out the ice cream, and spoons it into your mouth if you're not aware that you're doing it. Have you ever noticed how this type of behavior can seem to happen either robotically or as if you're in some sort of trance? You are! You're in the trance of unawareness. Without awareness, there's no choice, only habitual reactions.

Unfortunately, even *with* awareness, sometimes it's hard to see choice, because the force of habit can be so great that it's stronger than the awareness. You can probably identify with the experience of doing something while being fully aware that you don't want the consequences of it, like hearing yourself say something harsh and unkind to your teenager while being unable to stop, as if it were someone else yelling. You know perfectly well that your words will only push your kid farther away and make her even more resistant to doing whatever it is she's not doing (or vice versa). Sometimes it feels like you're just channeling your father or mother, and it is just this feeling of helplessness that precipitates the spiral of emotions from frustration with your child, to frustration with yourself, to feelings like rage, despair, and extreme agitation.

In these cases, self-forgiveness and self-compassion are wonderful allies and friends. We'll explore this important subject in depth later, but for now let's just say that when there's clarity at the level of intentions and values, it's easier to recover and reestablish our commitments when we feel that wc'vc failed.

The Power of Intention

The most powerful and yet often invisible function of intention is the potential it has to affect outcome. For a sailor, it's quite obvious that the aim of the rudder has everything to do with the direction the boat sails. However, in our Western culture, we're trained to focus on actions as the sole determinants of outcomes and to ignore intention or motivation. This is exemplified in aphorisms like "The road to hell is paved with good intentions," or "Actions speak louder than words." Of course, if wholesome intentions are never reflected in concrete actions, the road to hell will indeed be smoothly paved! And yet, in other traditions, it's intention that plays the most important role in the consequences of our actions. There's a Tibetan saying—"Everything rests on the tip of intention."

A good example of this is in gift giving. Let's say you bought a scarf for a friend. If you give the scarf out of friendship and generosity, it will be received quite differently than if you offer it expecting something in return. Perhaps you want to be appreciated, maybe you're hoping to "buy" her affection, or maybe you want to be absolved for some prior misdeed. Same scarf, same act of giving, but the experience of receiving the gift can be quite different in each of these scenarios. The first-century Roman philosopher Seneca agreed with this view: "A gift consists not in what is done or given, but in the intention of the giver or doer." It's actually possible to slap someone with his best interests in mind. There are rare occasions when a slap may be the only way to prevent someone from harming himself or others or to disrupt a self-destructive cycle. A slap that is motivated by love and concern will be received entirely differently from a slap delivered in a fit of anger.

What Are Values? Why Do They Matter?

Personal values are the beliefs, principles, or ideas that are important to you in life. Values are things that you stand for, things that you believe in and are willing to support and fight for. (Or, in some cases, things that you oppose and are willing to fight against.) They provide a road map for the kind of life you aspire to lead.

In the last ten years, research has shown that the simple act of prioritizing values results in (1) reduced stress (Creswell et al. 2005); (2) strengthened willpower (Schmeichel and Vohs 2009); (3) increased openness and decreased bias (Correll, Spencer, and Zanna 2004); and (4) improved accuracy by reducing defensiveness (Legault, Al-Khindi, and Inzlicht 2012). The simple exercise of thinking and writing about what's really important in life has even been shown to be effective in weight loss. In 2012 researchers at the University of Waterloo (Ontario) and Stanford found that when they offered subjects (45 women) a simple writing exercise in "values affirmation," two and a half months later the control group reported an average weight gain of 2.76 pounds while those who completed the exercise lost an average of 3.4 pounds (Logel and Cohen 2012). Though a fairly small sample, these are stunning results from a simple, one-time writing exercise!

Although it's only relatively recently that psychology has begun to research the importance of values for psychological well-being, spiritual traditions have always emphasized the role that values play in leading a fulfilling and exemplary human life. On Zen retreats, there's a traditional *gatha* that's often recited at the end of a long day of intensive sitting meditation:

> Let me respectfully remind you:
> Life and death are of supreme importance.
> Time swiftly passes and opportunity is lost.
> Each of us must strive to awaken!
> This night your days will have diminished by one.
> Awaken, take heed; do not squander your life.

Many spiritual traditions have used reflections on death as "thought experiments" to inspire conscious living and the alignment of daily actions with one's deepest values. Don Juan, the shaman in the books of Carlos Castaneda, counseled his disciple to keep death on his left shoulder, as an adviser and constant reminder of what matters. As of April 2013, Pastor Rick Warren's book, *The Purpose Driven Life,* had sold over 60 million copies. The remarkable success of this book could be construed as evidence for our deep and abiding need to align our lives with our deepest values.

But assuming that all the world's great spiritual traditions agree with sources as divergent as Warren and Castaneda that values are foundational to leading a good and happy life, why isn't it easier to discover and follow them?

Values, Personal Ethics, and Emotional Balance

People who have a deep and abiding religious faith tend to find it easy to embrace the values and ethics that are suggested in their tradition. Others have a relationship with religion that is at best ambivalent and at worst antagonistic. These mixed or downright aversive feelings can significantly complicate our feelings about the values and mores of a particular religion. Depending on how unconscious these feelings are, they can undermine us in ways that range from hesitancy to paralysis or self-sabotage. Paradoxically, while most of the world's religions endorse values that we would all agree with—love, kindness, generosity, compassion—they have also, at times, tended to foster less desirable qualities, ranging from narrow-mindedness to outright hatred and cruelty. Yet if people rebel against religion because of these latter qualities, they may find themselves warring with their own deeply held values as well, and end up throwing out the proverbial baby (in this case qualities like compassion and kindness) with the bathwater (the Crusades, the Inquisition, or other examples of cruelty in the name of religion). Understanding this dilemma, His Holiness the Dalai Lama has used his worldwide popularity to endorse what he calls "secular ethics." Ethics can be understood as the actions that are derived from our values. He has often been quoted as saying: "My religion is kindness," and has been tireless in his efforts to promote compassion and kindness without the slightest agenda to convert anyone to Buddhism.

We'd like to propose that the foundation for this program is neither religious nor secular ethics; it's *personal* ethics. *These* values and ethics can only be understood in the crucible of your own heart and mind, and are not accepted on blind faith. This is the good news and the bad news. The good news is, there's no one to rebel against. The bad news is—you guessed it!—there's no one to rebel against. We often joke with students in our classes that we're not their mothers, their fathers, or their teachers. There are no grades and no guilt trips. No one will be disappointed if you don't follow through on these practices ... except you!

The more our choices line up with our values, the better we generally feel about ourselves. On the other hand, actions that don't align with personal values give rise to guilt, regret, agitation, worry, paranoia, mistrust, fear, and defensiveness. When not met with awareness, these feelings tend to get stored in an "invisible backpack" that we unconsciously carry everywhere we go. The heavier the invisible backpack, the more off-balance we become.

The concept of personal ethics can be understood in practical terms as well as holistic ones. In the fall of 2004, Margaret interviewed Marshall Rosenberg, who developed Nonviolent Communication (NVC), for the journal *Inquiring Mind.* The journal was interested in an interview with Marshall because so many mindfulness meditators were studying NVC at the time. When Margaret asked Marshall about this, and if he ever meditated, he replied: "I'm from Detroit, so I don't use the word meditation. I see it as getting my shit together. This means getting clear on how I choose to live before I go out in the world" (Cullen and Kabatznick 2004).

The less aligned your life is with your personal values, the more vulnerable you are to emotional imbalance. Let's refer again to the example of yelling when you come home from work. Had you clarified your intentions before walking in the door—perhaps reminding yourself of how much your family means to you, or setting a strong intention to be patient with your partner—chances are you would have been less reactive. On the other hand, had you failed to do this, and spoken harshly, chances are you would have felt out of sync with the person you would like to be, and this "integrity gap" would likely have given rise to feelings of unhappiness and disappointment.

In this workbook, we'll translate knowledge and ideas into firsthand experience. In the first few chapters, you were introduced to exercises using pen and paper. In this chapter we added an experiment about noticing the intention to move, and we'll also suggest a field observation regarding intentions. Finally, beginning with the following exercise, we'll add formal practices, some of which will include audio recordings. (You can download these recordings at http://www.newharbing er.com/28395—see the back of this book for detailed instructions.) We have intentionally used the language and metaphors of science for the interactive componentsin this workbook because we encourage you to become a scientist in the laboratory of your have intentionally used the language and metaphors of science for the interactive components in this workbook because we encourage you to become a scientist in the laboratory of your own heart and mind. Some of the best attitudes you can bring to this experience are curiosity, open-mindedness, honesty, integrity, humor, and kindness. These are helpful allies both in the lab and in your life.

Exercise 1: The Well

(*recording available at* http://www.newharbinger.com/28395)

The following guided visualization can be accessed on audio recording, or you can read the directions below and then lead yourself.

It's helpful to begin any session of guided visualization or meditation with three long, deep breaths. As you inhale, see if you can direct the breath all the way down into the belly and imagine filling up the whole torso with the in-breath, from the belly to the collar bones, just as you'd fill a vessel with water. Then, as you exhale, expel all of the air from the torso until you're actually pulling the belly button back toward the spine. If possible, allow the out-breath to be even longer than the in-breath. After the third exhalation, let the breath return to its natural rhythm.

Now, in your mind's eye, imagine an old-fashioned water well, the kind that goes deep into the earth, to the source of cool, fresh water. Take a moment to close your eyes and get a clear picture of the scene. There might be a grassy knoll, and perhaps a stone arch over the well with a wooden bucket. Notice the temperature, the sky, and any other particulars that can place you in the scene. In front of you, on the ground, is a lovely stone. You bend down and pick it up and feel the texture, temperature, shape, and weight of the stone in your hand. Because this is the world of the mind, where anything is possible, imagine that there's a question embedded in the heart of the stone: "Why am I reading this book? What am I hoping to get out of it? What is my heart yearning for?" As you toss the stone into the well, listen for the answer that splashes up as the stone breaks the surface of the water. And then, as the stone slowly finds its way down into the well, see if any other answers bubble up to the surface. Slowed by the density of the water, the stone might carom off the sides of the well, sending up different answers as it moves deeper down. Eventually, it settles on the bottom of the well. Listen to see if one more answer floats up to the surface to the question, "Why have I chosen this book?"

Write any answers that came to you.

Notes

_____

These answers can serve as a touchstone as you go through this book. Should resistance arise to doing the practice (big smile—it will!), it can help to return to your original intentions for reading this book. If you are hoping for equanimity, balance, peace of mind, and so on, remind yourself of these intentions as you go so they can support your resolve.

Exercise 2: The Three Questions

(*recording available at* http://www.newharbinger.com/28395)

This exercise, like most guided visualizations, works best if you can take a few minutes to collect and relax the mind. We first heard it from the Buddhist scholar and teacher B. Alan Wallace. Again, you might find it easier to listen to the guided meditation on the website associated with the book, but written directions follow. Either way, you are encouraged to write the answers to the questions in the spaces provided.

Start with the three breaths described above, and then imagine a beautiful place in nature, where you can lie on your back, on a blanket, and look up at the blue sky in all its vastness. Pick a spot where you can be perfectly comfortable, and create the conditions in your environment where your mind and body can relax and your senses can open. Again, it can be helpful to close your eyes for a few minutes in order to fully put yourself in the scene.

As you lie here, comfortably gazing at the sky in your mind's eye, reflect on the following three questions, waiting until the end to write down your answers:

1. If anything were possible, what would I love to receive from the world? Let your imagination be as wide as the sky and allow the answer to be

unedited. For now, there's no right or wrong answer, no need for embarrassment or correction.

---

2. If I could grow in any way, how would I love to develop in this lifetime? What qualities would I love to nurture?

---

3. If I could offer anything to the world, what would I love to offer? How would I like to contribute, and to be remembered? Again, allow this answer to be uncensored, in the privacy of your own heart and mind.

Feel free to return to these answers any time you need a dose of inspiration. It can also be helpful to revisit the questions from time to time, as a way to refresh your intentions and to notice what core values remain consistent over time.

Field Observation: Setting Intentions

The field observations are *intended* to be fun and simple ways to integrate the ideas and concepts in this book into everyday life. But please don't be deceived by how simple they seem. It's easy for the mind to dismiss what's simple and obvious as unworthy, but this couldn't be further from the truth.

This week, whenever you remember it, set a simple intention, based on the answers that came to you in the guided visualizations above. For example, you might decide you'd like to be kinder, more patient, more compassionate, or more generous. Your only job is to set the intention each morning. If it's helpful to you, write it on a sticky note and put it somewhere you can see it. But this isn't necessary. If you forget first thing in the morning, whenever you remember is fine! It's not your job to measure how well you did, just to set the intention.

Use the space provided to write down your intentions, as well as whatever you noticed during the day that might be an outcome of setting those intentions.

Field Notes

_____

Intentions are what drive thoughts, words, and actions. Even when we're not fully aware of our intentions, they effectively drive our actions and define their outcome. When unconscious, intentions tend to be a function of habit and conditioning rather than of the core values that we have chosen. These values, in turn, represent the important beliefs, principles, or ideas that you stand for, which guide your life. They reflect what you really care about and are willing to fight for.

Clarifying your intentions and aligning them with your core values is an important strategy for cultivating emotional balance because it reduces emotional reactivity and short-circuits the downward emotional spiral that can lead to feelings of being overwhelmed. And remembering and nourishing your personal values enhances psychological well-being and fosters resilience.

Though often associated with the domains of religion and philosophy, ethics can be religious, secular, or personal, depending on your values and faith tradition. Values evolve and transform over time—therefore it's important to keep an inner conversation that is alive, fresh, and open *about what really matters to you in life.*

Part 2

The Program

In this part of the book, you'll be embarking on an eight-week journey into greater happiness, freedom, and emotional balance. Each exercise, experiment, and practice is designed to support and deepen insights that have the potential to radically transform your life. For a few rare people, this transformation occurs dramatically like a strike of lightning. For most of us, it's gradual, almost imperceptible, like becoming wet from the fog rather than from a downpour. However these insights occur, it's rarely sufficient to have only an intellectual understanding. Just as reading a menu is not the same as tasting the food, reading about forgiveness is not the same as *forgiving.*

Before any program of change can be undertaken, it helps to start with reality. We are human, and always will be; flawed, beautiful, deep, yearning, complex, multidimensional, and dynamic. Expectations that are idealized and inconsistent with reality set the stage for failure and disappointment. Just consider the myth of "living happily ever after" and how utterly inconsistent this is with the reality of marriage. But when you inevitably fail to live up to your expectations, there *is* a refuge that you can always rely on: beginning again. Jack Kornfield captured this perfectly when he said, "We as humans have this amazing capacity to be reborn at breakfast every day and say 'This is a new day. Who will I be?'"

On a more pragmatic level, it helps a great deal to set up a quiet, inviting place to practice, where you can easily access the recordings and be relatively undisturbed, and to pick a time to practice each day—no matter what. For most people, getting up twenty minutes earlier each day is the easiest way to stay consistent.

Finally, because the business of finding emotional balance and cultivating mindfulness is serious, and may even be the most important thing you ever do, it's important to lighten up and find humor wherever possible. In the words of the writer Anne Lamott, "Laughter is carbonated holiness."

Chapter 4

Learning How to Pay Attention

ONE BREATH, ONE SENSATION AT A TIME

Once your intentions have been clarified, the next step toward cultivating mindfulness and emotional balance is the training of attention. Every contemplative practice requires the development of this skill, and, once learned in meditation, it can be deployed in daily life, where the rubber meets the road. Returning to the metaphor of the boat, the captain cannot successfully navigate the boat unless she is able to pay attention to all the conditions: the weather, the sea, the sky, and so on. If you're reading this book, most likely you're feeling tossed around by your feelings. Whether you're struggling with anxiety, anger, sadness, or fear, it's actually possible to feel relatively calm and collected, even amid these feelings. Attention is the key to this extraordinary claim.

In this chapter, we'll explore how attention can be trained using the breath and the body as the first base or *foundation* for mindfulness training. In fact, working with the breath is probably the most universally agreed upon method for emotion regulation.

But before going any further, let's start with a brief experiment.

Experiment: Noticing Your Breath

Without modifying your body posture or breathing pattern, bring awareness to how you're breathing right now. Observing without judgment, just as a lab scientist would observe a natural phenomenon, notice how you're breathing. Is your breath deep or shallow? Long or short? Are you breathing through your mouth or your nostrils? Take sixty seconds to observe this. Where do you feel your breath most prominently? Maybe you feel it in your chest or your belly; or perhaps the sensations of your breath are more prominent in your nostrils or your throat. Take another sixty seconds to observe the sensations of the breath, and write down some notes about what you observed.

Notes

Attention: The Muscle That Powers Everything

Most people would agree that very little can be accomplished in life, let alone during meditation, without the ability to pay attention. In a tragically misguided attempt to get as much accomplished as possible, we often pride ourselves on how many tasks we can manage at the same time. Recently, research has begun to tell us what meditation masters have known for millennia: multitasking is a myth; we can only really pay attention to one thing at a time (Wang and Tchernev 2012). To pay attention should be like breathing—natural, effortless, and uncontrived. Yet directing attention where we'd like it to go, and sustaining it for any length of time, isn't so easy. After all, were you ever taught how to pay attention? Or even what attention *is?*

In 1890, psychologist and philosopher William James described attention as

> the taking possession by the mind, in clear and vivid form, of one out of what seem several simultaneously possible objects or trains of thought. Focalization, concentration, of consciousness are of its essence. It implies withdrawal from some things in order to deal effectively with others, and is a condition which has a real opposite in the confused, dazed, scatterbrained state. (James 1890, 403–4)

James referred to the importance of attention in our lives in the following terms:

> [T]he faculty of voluntarily bringing back a wandering attention, over and over again, is the very root of judgment, character, and will. No one is *compos sui* [master of himself] if he have it

not. An education which should improve this faculty would be the education *par excellence.* But it is easier to define this ideal than to give practical directions for bringing it about. (James 1890, 424)

He is, of course, absolutely right. Most of us were never offered practical directions for paying attention. Even in this era of tutoring, workshops, and self-help, we've never seen a course in "paying attention." This is exactly where meditation comes in.

How Do We Train Attention?

The best place to begin the training of attention is by focusing on the sensations created by the breath in the body. In Buddhism, mindfulness of the body is the first of the "four foundations of mindfulness"—the other three being mindfulness of feelings, mind, and the dharma (the natural law of the unfolding of phenomena).

There are several practical reasons to choose the breath as the initial base for attentional training. First, the sensations of the breath are relatively more concrete and tangible than feelings, thoughts, and emotions, which makes it easier to use them as an anchor to bring back attention over and over again. Bringing attention to the breath also moves attention out of the head, allowing access to a different, more physical and experiential perspective.

The breath, which is present as long as you're alive, tends to be a fairly neutral object, evoking strong feelings neither of liking nor of disliking, and this neutrality makes it easier to steady the mind. Though they may be more or less subtle, there are always sensations associated with the expansion of the in-breath and the contraction of the out-breath. Under most circumstances, you don't have to exert any effort in order to breathe. The breath also provides a subtle bridge of integration and balance between several pairs of opposites: mental activity and bodily states; voluntary and involuntary body functions; and sympathetic (fight or flight) and parasympathetic (rest and digest) branches of the autonomic nervous system.

Last but not least, the breath is the simplest, quickest, and often most accessible strategy for regulating emotion. It's usually pretty obvious that the breath becomes quicker and more shallow with challenging emotions such as fear and anger. And we've all been told to stop and take a few long, deep breaths to regain composure when we're caught in the grip of a strong emotion. And sure enough, two or three long, slow, deep breaths are often sufficient to ride the crest of a powerful feeling.

Okay, so we know what to do, and we know that it works, so where's the problem? It may be that it's hard to remember to actually do it, because the mind and body are primed to perpetuate the emotion. It could also be that we're deceived by the simplicity of this strategy—dismissing it as too obvious or not mighty enough to meet the challenge of our current state. Whatever the reason, mindfulness of breathing not only helps to train attention, but strengthens the neural pathway that remembers to focus on the breath, thus making this strategy more available when we're feeling tossed about or out of control.

Exercise: Mindfulness of Breathing

Find a posture that allows you to be both relaxed and alert. Straighten your spine a little bit, gently roll your shoulders back and down, opening the chest and relaxing the belly. Begin with three deep, cleansing breaths. After the third exhalation, allow the breath to return to its own natural rhythm. With as much patience and kindness as you can muster, focus your attention on the sensations of expansion and contraction in the belly as you breathe. As best as you can, let go of all control of the breath, letting it be deep or shallow, rough or smooth, fast or slow. Imagine your attention riding the waves of the breath just as a boat rides the waves of the sea, staying connected to the whole arc of the wave from the peak to the trough. Do this for three to five minutes.

After you finish, reflect on the following questions: Did you notice any change in your body or mind after practicing breath awareness for a couple of minutes? Did the mind stay focused on the breath the whole time? Did it wander off to fantasies, memories, plans, images, or other mental contents? Write down your answers to these questions below.

Notes

_____

When trying this seemingly simple exercise for the first time, people are typically surprised by how busy their minds are. If you had trouble feeling one whole in-breath before your mind slipped away, you're in good company. Traditional texts in Buddhism about the first stages of attentional training compare the mind to a cascading waterfall. In the Indian Yoga tradition, the image is less poetic but more amusing: the untrained mind is like a drunken monkey, jumping from one branch to the next while a scorpion stings its tail.

Here we come to a very important point about mindfulness training we cannot stress enough: the single biggest obstacle to meditation is the mistaken belief that mind-wandering is a problem that needs to be fixed. Yes, you got it right—mind-wandering is *not* a problem! It's simply the nature of mind. Our minds manufacture thoughts; that's their job. Meditation doesn't "buy their product," so this may cause them to try even harder, manufacturing not only more thoughts, but sexier and more seductive ones.

Attention is trained by bringing awareness back to the breath whenever you become aware that the mind has wandered off. In this way, each time the mind wanders, a new opportunity to train attention presents itself, that same capacity that is "the very root of judgment, character, and will," as William James put it. Thus, there are three reiterative steps in the process of training the mind to pay attention to a chosen object (such as the breath, or bodily sensations); and in this process, getting distracted is not an obstacle, but actually what allows us to build the muscle of attention:

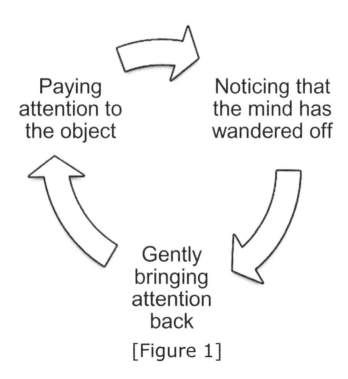

[Figure 1]

As you cycle through these steps many times—perhaps hundreds of times—during a meditation period, it's crucial to keep a nonjudgmental and friendly attitude toward yourself. Ideas of perfection, success, and failure simply don't work here because you can't force your mind into obedient stillness. Meditation is like training a puppy. How would you relate to a puppy who excitedly runs off here and there when you're training it to stay? If you respond with anger, judgment, and impatience, the puppy will not trust you and will fear and resent you, but if you treat it with patience, humor, love, and firm guidance, you're more likely not only to see the results you want, but also to win a loyal friend.

The mind, too, is a very sensitive animal. Therefore, training the mind requires the same wise, friendly, and firm attitude. Just as you wouldn't take the puppy's responses personally, it's wise not to take your own mind personally, remembering that mind-wandering is a universal phenomenon. According to some researchers, mind-wandering takes up 47 percent of our waking life (Killingsworth and Gilbert 2010); other researchers have estimated that our minds produce between 12,000 and 70,000 thoughts a day. In fact, not surprisingly, research is now showing that mind-wandering is our brain's default mode network (Hasenkamp et al. 2012).

So ... it's not *your mind,* it's just *the nature of mind.* Simply include wandering mind in the meditation, instead of fighting it as something bad that should stay out of the meditation room. Noticing the breath, noticing the mind wandering, and gently bringing the mind back are all equally important components of training attention.

Bearing these strategies in mind, let's go back to the last exercise and try it again. Set your watch or timer for another three minutes and see how it goes.

How was it this time?

Reclaiming Your Living Body

Although breath awareness will be the basis for almost all the meditation practices that you will learn in this program, the home practice for this week will focus on paying attention to bodily sensations through the practice of the body scan.

The body scan is a very important practice. On one level, it will help you train attentional skills by bringing awareness to physical sensations over and over again. On a deeper level, this profoundly healing practice will help you reconnect with your body and reinhabit it from within.

We live in a culture in which the body tends to be neglected. From a moralistic age in which the body was conceived as a prison for the soul and the source of all sin, we're now shifting to a highly technological era in which our virtual lives seem to be taking more space than our real lives. Spending many hours seated in front of screens in often harmful postures, we can become quite disconnected from our bodies. And when we don't listen to our bodily sensations, we become unable to read the messages they're trying to communicate. In a way, an unattended sensation is like a letter we've sent ourselves but never opened.

In Margaret's work with cancer patients, it's heartbreaking to see how much suffering is added to the already considerable challenge of the disease and its treatment through self-condemnation and self-blame. Feelings of guilt, betrayal, and self-hatred are, for many people, more painful than the travails of chemo and radiation. Hundreds of cancer patients have gone through the program that you are embarking on and we've been amazed, time and again, at the power of mindfulness to relieve the mental and emotional suffering that is "added" to the experience of cancer.

Quite often, when people realize they need to pay attention to their bodies, they tend to view the body from the *outside in,* mainly focusing on its image and appearance. From this perspective, the body is seen as an object in need of some sort of adjustment or improvement: reduce body fat, increase aerobic capacity, change hair color, and so on. In that way, the body becomes an "it" or a thing that has to be manipulated. In mindfulness practices, we are doing quite the opposite: every mindfulness practice is an *embodied practice,* an approach to experience from the *inside out* in which the lived experience of the body is brought into focus.

Francisco Varela—a noted molecular biologist and contemplative who cofounded the Mind and Life

Institute—was fond of using a distinction found in the German language that reflects these two approaches to the body, a distinction that is absent in English. The German word *Körper* refers to the body as a structure or object, and is used when referring to a corpse or someone else's body. In contrast, *Leib* refers to the living body of direct experience, the body of sensations and feelings through which we live. It's not a coincidence that the word *Leib* resembles the English term "life," since they share the same root—*lif* in Old English, meaning a "person-self constituted by the quality of being a life." Notice the contrast with the word "body," which comes from the Old English *bodig,* meaning "barrel" or "cask."

By practicing mindful awareness of our bodily sensations, we actively reclaim our bodies as a precious dimension of life (even during a serious illness), slowly learning to tune into our experience and move away from the objectification and manipulation of ourselves.

Practice Plan, Week 1

Meditation Practice: The Body Scan

(*recording available at* http://www.newharbinger.com /28395)

This is the first formal mindfulness practice you will learn in this program. You can practice the body scan on your own by using the following written instructions or by listening to the audio instructions. Whenever possible, we encourage you to follow the audio guidance, since it rarely works to read a meditation and then memorize it sufficiently to do it on your own. The general suggestion for each practice in this part of the book is to do it regularly, ideally once a day for a whole week, before moving to the next chapter or practice. If this isn't possible for you, try to practice as often as possible. Remember that what you get from the practices depends on your commitment to them.

The body scan is an important mindfulness practice because it allows you to become more aware of what is going on within the body on a moment-to-moment basis, and lets you get away from the nearly constant thinking, judging, and other processes that occur solely within the head.

Some people find the body scan to be very relaxing, and it's quite common to fall asleep at various points in this practice. Whether you relax or not, keep in mind that this is not a relaxation exercise, but an awareness practice in which we're training the mind to pay close attention to present-moment experience in a nonjudgmental way. In the body scan, you won't contract and then relax muscles as in some relaxation techniques. The body scan is simply about bringing awareness to how the body feels in the present moment, without trying to change anything.

If you're able to lie down without going to sleep, lie down on your back with your arms about 45 degrees from your body (palms up) and a pillow under your head and knees if needed for comfort. Or you might prefer to do the body scan sitting upright, with an erect spine. Allow your eyes to gently close.

- Begin by bringing attention to your left toes. Notice any sensations that exist in your toes. It's so common to take the toes for granted, not even noticing that they're there unless they hurt. Draw attention to however they feel right now, in this present moment, without judging or trying to change anything. If you do notice that the sensations in your toes change, be aware of that change without trying to control it.

- Now, shifting attention to the top of your left foot, bring awareness to however it feels right now, drawing attention to any sensations that arise, such as the feeling of your skin against your socks, or sensations of temperature, pressure, tension, tingling, itching, and so on.

- Each time you find the mind wandering from the body part you're focusing on, acknowledge that it has wandered and gently return the attention to the body. When you do this, don't give yourself a hard time or get angry with yourself for not focusing; simply return the mind to the body in a nonjudgmental way as you continue with the body scan.

- Slowly progress in this way throughout the body, going up the left leg to the pelvis, and then up the right leg, beginning with the right toes. Then shift attention to various parts of the torso, abdomen, lower back, upper back, chest, and shoulders. Go down each arm to the fingertips, and then move up the neck and throat to all areas of the face. Conclude with the back and then the top of the head.

- As you go through the body, there's no need to make anything special happen. Most of what you notice will be quite ordinary: pressure, contact, tingling, warmth, coolness, itching, softness, stiffness, heaviness, lightness, and so forth. If a part of the body has no sensation, just notice this, perhaps using a mental label like "numb" or "blank." If there's pain or other strong sensations in other parts of the body, acknowledge the experience and gently escort your attention back to the part of the body that is the focus of the body scan.

- Allow your attention to linger at the top of the head, and then expand your sphere of awareness to include your breathing. Imagine yourself breathing throughout your entire body, beginning at the top of your head and extending all the way to your fingers and toes. As you breathe in, allow the air to fill your body. As you breathe out, allow the air to exit from your entire body.

- Invite yourself to remain in this state of stillness for a few moments.

- As you're ready, return awareness to the entire body, beginning to move your feet and hands. You might then want to move your arms and legs, stretch, or rock from side to side on your back.

- Gently open your eyes and return your awareness to the room.

The Body Scan—FAQs

Below are some comments and questions people commonly share after their first body scan, with some answers that may prove useful. We strongly encourage you to actually do the practice at least once before reading the questions and answers, so that you can relate them to your own experience. Some questions and answers will not resonate with your experience, and that's perfectly fine.

- "I kept thinking about other things and had trouble focusing on my body."

  - This is a very common occurrence, because it's the nature of the mind to think and wander. This is where a nonjudgmental attitude is so helpful; without criticizing or getting upset with yourself, just notice that the mind has wandered and then return your focus to the body. This is a normal part of the practice and doesn't mean that you've done anything wrong. Actually, it's not possible to control what enters the mind, but it is possible to train your mind so that there's more control over what happens next, which in turn establishes the habit of returning the focus nonjudgmentally to the body.

- "I was distracted by pain in my _____ (leg, neck, etc.)."

  - This is also a very common situation. Some people have ongoing pain that's brought more acutely to their attention during the body scan, while others notice pains they have never felt before. How did you relate to that pain? Frequently, there's aversion to both physical pain and mental distraction, and this aversion tends to increase the pain and give rise to yet more discursive thinking. When you notice that something is painful, see if you can continue to bring your attention back to the part of the body the instruction is focusing on. Even if you have to keep returning your focus over and over, this is a helpful part of the practice. Don't ignore or try to suppress the pain, just notice that it's calling your attention and then, as best you can, return your attention to the other part of your body. Once the body scan arrives at the painful part, remain open to whatever sensations you may experience. See if you can breathe in and out of this area, curiously observing how the sensations of pain may change. Then, as the body scan progresses, continue on to the next part of the body.

- "What if there's a part of my body I can't feel?"

  • Just notice that you're not feeling anything, and maintain awareness of this "nonfeeling" without judging yourself or trying to feel something that's not there. Remember that the practice is not about creating any special or different sensations, and that whatever you experience at each moment is just as it should be in this practice. Finally, sometimes sensations are ignored or dismissed because they're too obvious or simple, like the feel of clothing on the skin or a sense of heaviness from gravity. As you continue practicing regularly, see if your attention sharpens, allowing you to perceive these subtler sensations.

- "What should I do if I just keep falling asleep?"

  • Sleepiness is also very common during the body scan. Everything you experience during the body scan can be viewed as information your body is giving you. Perhaps you haven't been getting enough sleep, or maybe this isn't the ideal time of day to be doing this type of practice. Regardless of the reason for your sleepiness, accept today's body scan practice just as it was, without being hard on yourself or judging your "performance." Sleepiness is one of the major hindrances that most meditators face eventually, and there are many strategies for working with it. You can try sitting up, opening your eyes, taking a few deep breaths, or becoming curious about it (energy tends to follow curiosity). You can even play a game with yourself to see if you can notice at what part of the body you tend to fall asleep. Keeping it light and playful never hurts!

- "I felt restless and agitated."

    • Restlessness is the other main challenge. There are different strategies for working with restlessness. You can try taking a few deep breaths and see if there are muscles in the body that can be consciously relaxed. Often, agitation is fueled by resisting some aspect of experience. See if you're fighting with the thinking mind, or if there's a painful feeling lurking under the surface you might be avoiding, such as sadness or fear. Remember, it's not a problem for the mind to become distracted, and you don't need to get rid of thoughts. Just notice "thinking," and escort the attention back to the body, allowing the thoughts to leave by themselves.

- "I was distracted by strong feelings of sadness, anger, fear..."

    • The strategies suggested above for working with restlessness and agitation can help when strong emotions arise during the body scan. Without suppressing the emotion or getting lost in the story of what happened, try to notice and name the feeling, and then bring your attention back to the body. Later on, we'll explore how to bring mindfulness to the emotions themselves.

Practice Log

For each day that you practice the body scan, fill in the following log. Keeping track of your insights with the practices will help you integrate what you learn from your experience over time. You can find additional copies of this log at http://www.newharbin ger.com/28395.

Date and time	What did I notice in my experience with this practice?

Field Observation: Notice the quality of your breath

Notice the quality of your breath in everyday life. As many times a day as you remember, do a quick check-in with your own breath. Is your breath long or short? Deep or shallow? Are your chest and shoulders open or closed? Is your breathing pattern related in any way to how you're feeling? If so, how?

Field Notes

_____

Field Observation: Be present in small ways

Pick one small daily activity and see if you can devote your full attention to it. It could be brushing your teeth, putting on your shoes, cutting vegetables, taking a shower, or walking from the parking lot to your office. Whatever you choose, see if you can bring the same kind and patient attention to the wandering mind that you would bring to the breath-awareness practice. Whenever you notice your attention is elsewhere, bring it back to the simple sensations in the body that accompany the activity.

Field Notes

_____

Attention is the ability to focus your mind voluntarily on a chosen object. It is a fundamental skill that is necessary for any kind of effective learning. The capacity to pay attention is crucial for emotional balance, since it gives you the freedom to focus your mind in constructive ways, instead of being tossed around by random internal or external stimuli.

The breath and the body are excellent places to begin training attention through the practices of breath awareness and the body scan. One of the biggest obstacles of attention training is the false belief that mind-wandering is a problem that needs to be fixed. Mind-wandering is a natural phenomenon, and becoming aware of it is an important step in attentional training.

The body scan and other embodied mindfulness practices allow us to reconnect with the experience of being alive and to recognize that the body is not a mere object. From this chapter on we encourage you to develop a regular practice. This is the best way to obtain the desired benefits from this program.

Chapter 5

Feelings: Pleasant, Unpleasant, and Neutral

WHERE ALL THE TROUBLE BEGINS

"Feeling tones" can be described as the *flavors* that accompany each moment of experience, whether received from the five senses (sight, sound, smell, taste, and touch) or from the mind—sometimes referred to as the sixth sense since it also "perceives" mental experiences. This implies that there aren't only pleasant, unpleasant, and neutral sounds, smells, or tastes, but also pleasant, unpleasant, and neutral thoughts, memories, and plans.

In Buddhist philosophy, feeling tones are the second of the four foundations of mindfulness mentioned earlier. The foundations are domains of experience to which it's particularly useful to pay mindful attention in order to liberate the mind from greed, hatred, and delusion. It turns out that at least two of these three "poisons," as they are often called, are also significant culprits in emotional turmoil. Chances are, if you're feeling distressed you're either wanting something you *don't* have (greed) or not wanting something you *do* have (hatred, or aversion). Paying attention to feeling tones, subtle though they are, can be a powerful tool to prevent emotional overload.

Bringing mindful awareness to pleasant experiences weakens the tendency to grasp onto them and crave more of them. Similarly, when we focus on unpleasant feeling tones, rather than on the discomfort itself, the tendency to push away and resist is diminished. Either way, emotional reactivity can be nipped in the bud before it becomes overwhelming. If you managed to set some time aside and explore the body scan practice suggested in the previous chapter even once, you might have noticed that whatever arises in your moment-to-moment experience—bodily sensations, fleeting thoughts, plans, memories, bursts of emotion, inner commentary, silence, and so on—comes with a sticky note attached that says "pleasant," "unpleasant," or "neutral." This happens so fast it often occurs below the threshold of awareness. Though we're rarely aware of this instant and continuous evaluation of experience when caught up in the busyness of life, our bodies and minds are well trained to react to these evaluations.

It could be argued that these feeling tones originally served an evolutionary function by repelling us from that which was toxic and attracting us to that which was beneficial to our survival. In fact, much of the food people find especially pleasant is loaded with fat and calories, which naturally made it very attractive for bodies and brains that evolved while having to obtain their energy from wild plants and animals. (We actually did this for 90 percent of our human history!) Those feeling tones helped us both to navigate potential dangers and to discern opportunities.

Experiment: Unpleasant, Pleasant, and Neutral

For the next sixty seconds, see if you can notice any experience that *does not* have a feeling tone associated with it—even a neutral one.

Any luck?

Take another sixty seconds and notice if your experiences tend to be mostly pleasant, unpleasant, or neutral, or equally divided among the three possibilities.

What did you notice?

Notes

_____

It's pretty easy to recognize the feelings of pleasant and unpleasant when they're strong, like a delicious dessert (pleasant!) or the smell of an open sewer (unpleasant!). But what about subtler moments of experience, like a fleeting thought of dessert (pleasant) or a vague sense of restlessness (unpleasant)? And what about all those moments that are neither pleasant nor unpleasant, such as putting on your socks or refilling the cat's bowl? In this chapter we'll explore how all these moments have the potential to spiral into emotional distress, as well as to inform behavior and choices that directly impact our sense of well-being.

By zooming in on this subtle level of experience, we'll explore a way to cultivate happiness that moves away from chasing the pleasant and avoiding the unpleasant—which some happiness researchers call *the hedonic treadmill.* The strategy proposed here, instead, consists of cultivating a mindful and spacious attitude with which to embrace all experience. But for now, feel free to keep a healthy dose of skepticism as you roll up your sleeves and explore this subject for yourself.

Exercise: The Power of Feeling Tones

This exercise has three steps. After reading the instructions for the first step, take a moment to close your eyes, do the exercise, and then jot down a few notes about your experience in the table below. Then continue with the remaining two steps of the exercise.

1. Begin with a few deep and diaphragmatic breaths. Take your time. Now, remember a time that was very pleasant, and let the memory get as strong as it can. Elaborate the memory in any way you can to make it as wonderful as possible. Focus on, and even exaggerate, the pleasant thoughts, feelings, and sensations that accompany this experience. Look for emotions such as joy, contentment, love, and

peacefulness. If other unrelated or unpleasant thoughts and feelings arise, gently bring your attention back to the good feelings evoked by this happy memory. Notice how it feels in your body. What is your mind like when you dwell on a happy memory? How does your heart feel? What do you feel motivated to do? After focusing on this experience for a minute or two, take a moment to write down what came up in your experience in the first row of the table below. Include bodily sensations that you noticed, thoughts and emotions that were prominent, and any motivations to act you might have noticed.

2. Take a few more deep breaths to "cleanse the palate" of the mind. Now, bring to mind an unpleasant memory—something that you feel *unhappy* about. Again, let this memory or visualization become as strong as you feel comfortable allowing it to grow. Remember that you are in charge and in complete control, since this is just a mental experiment. If it feels okay for you, exaggerate the most unpleasant aspects of the experience so that you can get a strong sense of them in your heart, mind, and body. There is tremendous power and freedom in strengthening the capacity to turn toward the difficult. Often, unpleasant memories involve emotions like anger, fear, shame, and grief. Is there resistance in switching from a pleasant to an unpleasant memory? How does that resistance manifest itself? Can you

locate it in the mind or the body? Do you notice any contraction or pulling back from this experience? Again, take a minute to write down a few words in the table below about the bodily sensations, thoughts, emotions, and motivations to act that came up for you.

3. Take a few more deep, diaphragmatic breaths, letting go of the previous experience and releasing the feelings associated with it. Now, see if you can bring to mind a memory that is neither particularly pleasant nor unpleasant—like getting the mail, or drying off after a shower. Choose something specific and see if you can bring this memory to mind as vividly as possible. How does this feel in the mind, heart, and body? Is it hard to get involved with the visualization? Does it feel less compelling because it doesn't have a strong charge, one way or another? What does your mind tend to do when experiences are neutral? Is it harder to stay present? See if you find any particular bodily sensations, thoughts, emotions, or impulses to act and jot them down in a few words in the last row of the table.

	Bodily Sensations	Emotions	Thoughts	Action
1. Pleasant Memory				
2. Unpleasant Memory				
3. Neutral Memory				

Before going deeper into an exploration of feeling tones, notice how, by simply paying attention and identifying thoughts, emotions, and physical sensations—as in the exercise you just did, or during a mindfulness practice—awareness naturally kicks in. When this happens, it becomes possible to *observe* experience instead of *identifying* with it. If the mind is trained to observe a thought as a thought, an emotion as an emotion, or a sensation as a sensation, the opportunity arises to observe and experience these phenomena from a spacious and nonreactive perspective.

Pleasant Experiences

There's a natural tendency to want to *cling to experiences that appear pleasant.* This clinging can actually diminish the pleasure of these experiences, as sadness or frustration arises when we realize that these experiences cannot last forever. Even if they lasted forever, they would soon turn into something unpleasant. (How much of that chocolate cake can you eat before it makes you sick? How much hot stone massage can you have before it turns into sophisticated torture?) Bringing awareness to the pleasant feeling tone diminishes the unconscious tendency to cling by revealing the fleeting and ever-changing nature of all experience. We have a natural tendency to delude ourselves into believing that pleasant experiences can be made permanent or that *just this time* we can cling to the pleasant without paying the price of suffering when it doesn't last. And yet we do this all the time.

Any time we're shocked or surprised by that which is unpleasant—whatever form it takes—also reveals a moment of clinging and delusion. We all know, for example, that the nature of the body is to get sick at times, to grow old, and eventually to die. Yet so often sickness is experienced as a mistake, a shock, or something out of the natural order. Any time the mind says "This shouldn't be happening" is a hint that there is delusion born of clinging. It's amazing how someone who is extremely rational and logical in most ways can nonetheless cling to a view that defies reason: "Parents always love their children unconditionally." "Partners never cheat on each other." "Children always love their parents." "Children shouldn't die." And the list goes on. These are myths that are clung to by intelligent people despite overwhelming evidence to the contrary. Why? Because of the power of attachment and clinging.

Bringing awareness to pleasant feeling tones can also reveal subtler and more reliable sources of happiness. Though the advertising industry would have us believe otherwise, moments of true happiness often share some or all of the following elements (none of which can be bought in a store):

- Connectedness (with self, others, or nature)

- Lack of expectation or demand

- Appreciation (of self or others)

- Savoring of simple pleasures

It can be illuminating to pay careful attention to the true sources of pleasure and happiness in life. How connected are they with the tremendous efforts we make to acquire and achieve? How connected are they to the moments of sense pleasure? When there is emotional distress, it becomes particularly important to understand what leads to happiness and what leads to unhappiness. The downward spirals of emotional distress are often fueled by the pursuit of relief through sense pleasures which leaves us only more and more unhappy and unfulfilled. Unfortunately, this is a common scenario.

Our culture "sells" happiness and peace of mind in the form of products. Just take a look at the ads you see in newspapers and magazines. We're constantly bombarded with the idea that to find happiness we have only to buy a bigger car, a better phone, or a better body through liposuction. We may think, "If I can just get all my ducks in a row, it will all be okay." Advertising has even caught on to the fact that consumers are now craving peace of mind even more than sense pleasures. More and more ads are selling "enlightenment" with their products.

Consider the following ad from the large department store chain, Nordstrom: An extremely attractive young man—not a day over twenty years old—is leaning on his elbows and appears to be lost in a fantasy as he looks out a window at the sea. He's wearing a nice-looking, understated V-neck sweater. On the opposite page, the caption reads: "I am inspired by the simple things. The bright white of the sand, the warmth of the sun, the sureness of the sea, the serenity of the waves. I have matured. I surround myself with people I love, things I truly need [the V-neck sweater, for example]. Finally, I am enlightened."

Wow, the sweater wasn't even that expensive. Love, serenity, even *enlightenment,* can be yours for a mere $59.95 and you even get a nice sweater in the bargain. What is fascinating, sad, and frightening about this is the idea that even peace of mind has been co-opted by the advertising industry. There are beautiful blondes sitting in full lotus with eyes closed on the backs of pickup trucks for automotive ads, and credit card companies that sell "enlightenment" as part of their campaigns.

There's a wonderful story from the Sufi tradition about the wise man fool, Mullah Nasruddin, that goes something like this: One evening, Nasruddin was on his hands and knees searching for something under a streetlamp. A man saw him and asked, "What are you looking for?" "My house key," Nasruddin replied. "I lost it." The man joined him in looking for the key, and after a period of fruitless searching, the man asked, "Are you sure you lost it around here?" Nasruddin replied, "Oh, I didn't lose it around here. I lost it over there, by my house." "Then why," the man asked, "are you looking for it over here?" "Because," Nasruddin said, "the light is so much better over here."

The advertising industry is like the streetlamp in the Nasruddin story, shining a bright and constant light in places where we'll never find what we're looking for.

Unpleasant Experiences

Similar to the tendency to cling to the pleasant, there is the opposite tendency to *push away things that appear unpleasant.* This can happen on both a gross and a subtle level. On a gross level, you might have a difficult day at work and go out drinking at night in order to numb yourself. On a more subtle level, you might have a fleeting thought about a comment someone made last week that left you feeling uneasy and forage in the refrigerator without being fully conscious of either the thought or the volition to get up and look in the fridge. However, distracting the mind from, avoiding, or "burying" unpleasant emotions, thoughts, or physical sensations often ends up intensifying these unpleasant experiences or making them manifest themselves in other forms, such as physical or mental health symptoms. Though not always easy, it can be a more effective approach to welcome unpleasant experiences as part of a full, rich life and view them with compassion and curiosity. No matter how well you line up your ducks, there will still be unpleasant feelings. They are your lived experience in the moment, and turning toward them is the doorway to freedom.

Typically, when discomfort—whether physical or emotional—is experienced, we label it as "bad." One subtle but important shift that can result from simply changing the labels to "pleasant, unpleasant, and neutral" is that there is less contraction around the difficult. This contraction, which instinctively arises in response to anything unpleasant, often gives rise to both thoughts and feelings that perpetuate and escalate distress. Let's take a common example and play it out in two ways. The first time, we'll respond habitually, without awareness, and see what happens. The second time, we'll bring mindfulness to the unpleasant experience.

Take something ordinary, like back pain. Many people experience back pain, for a variety of reasons. Often, a moment of back pain arises and, rather than simply noting it as "unpleasant sensation," the mind contracts around the experience. There might be a thought like "I hate this," or "I'm falling apart." That simple thought creates resistance in the body, and the sensation intensifies. This gives rise to more thoughts, such as "I'll have to cancel that hike," or "I'll never be able to play tennis again," or other extreme, distorted perceptions. These thoughts give rise to emotions, such as frustration or anger. With these emotions comes more tension, and the discomfort intensifies further. In real time, this happens quite fast and is a common pathway to emotional overload.

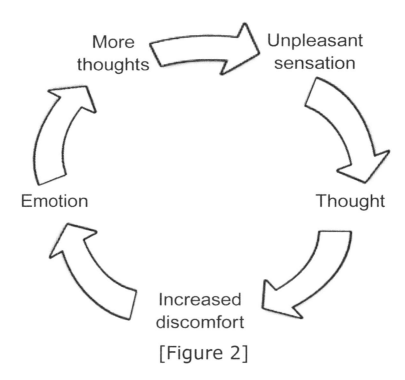

More thoughts · Unpleasant sensation · Thought · Increased discomfort · Emotion

[Figure 2]

There are some common misunderstandings around this way of relating to pain and difficulty. First, and perhaps most relevant for someone who experiences emotional distress, is the distinction between awareness of feelings and indulging in feelings. Western psychology has contributed to this confusion by promoting, at times and in certain schools, the strong expression of difficult emotions. In the early 1970s a psychologist named Arthur Janov developed something called "Primal Therapy," which promoted emotional catharsis. Yet subsequent research has shown that this method of dealing with strong emotions is ineffectual. In the case of anger in particular, expressing the emotion seems to increase it rather than make it more manageable. As we saw in chapter 2, emotions share the same nature of all phenomena: they are impermanent. But when frustration or discomfort arises and we "tell the story of it" over and over again, the story gets stuck.

If, however, a moment of back pain arises and it's simply noted as "unpleasant sensation," or more specifically, as something like "pressure" or "heat," that experience is now free to follow its natural course of arising and passing away. Even in the case of chronic pain, no sensation is permanent; and it can be quite liberating to see that even this shoulder that has been problematic for years is not a monolithic block of discomfort, but actually a complex experience of ever-changing sensations, and that there might be moments of ease within the chronic condition. This is even more the case with emotional distress. Emotions are designed to arise and pass away quickly, and when seen with mindful clarity, they tend to do just that!

Unpleasant experiences may have important life lessons to teach, or they may communicate messages from the body about health concerns that need attending to. When experienced without judgment, unpleasant experiences may change to neutral, or even pleasant, experiences. Sometimes, just the confidence that comes from facing difficulties can transform the unpleasant into the pleasant. When a particularly unpleasant emotion arises, such as shame or anxiety, finding the courage to "dive" into that emotion allows it to express its impermanent nature and also often results in the "pleasant" experience of your own profound bravery.

Neutral Experiences

When an experience seems neutral or uninteresting, *there is a tendency to tune out or ignore what's going on.* For example, there may be people in your life you encounter on a regular basis whom you neither like nor dislike—a coworker in your office, a neighbor, a janitor in your building, the cashier in the grocery store. These are people who draw little attention one way or the other. How do you respond to these people? Do they get as much attention as people whom you really like or dislike? How might your impression of these folks shift if you directed more of your attention toward them? Might you feel more empathy and compassion?

Often, turning attention toward a neutral experience changes the neutral character of its tone. Bringing focused attention to otherwise bland experiences can transform the neutral into the pleasant. In chapters 9 and 11, you will be practicing kindness and compassion meditations. Each of these involves directing caring feelings toward a "neutral" person. Invariably, after doing these practices for only a week, students come back reporting that they fell in love with, say, the dry cleaner or the bus driver. This is beautifully depicted in the novel *The Elegance of the Hedgehog,* by Muriel Barbery (2008), where the precocious (and suicidal) preteen Paloma begins to pay attention and slowly discovers the rich inner life of Renée, the apparently uninteresting concierge of her building—an encounter that eventually awakens in Paloma an appreciation for her own life.

The simple but powerful practice of noticing neutral events results in the savoring and reclaiming of simple things like walking, breathing, watching leaves fall from trees, drinking a cup of tea. The German poet Rainer Maria Rilke once wrote to a young poet: "If your everyday life seems poor, don't blame *it;* blame yourself; admit to yourself that you are not enough of a poet to call forth its riches; because for the creator there is no poverty and no poor, indifferent place" (Rilke 1984, 7). By harnessing the power of awareness through mindfulness practice, and embracing all of life's experiences, we can slowly learn to call forth life's riches—even from moments of distress and discomfort.

Relating to Feelings Mindfully

Paradoxically, one of the biggest obstacles to true happiness is treating unpleasant emotions as obstacles. This moment of aversion, of pushing away the unpleasant, is where the war begins. It's also the beginning of the slippery slope to emotional distress. It's actually possible to embrace every emotion and every experience—pleasant, unpleasant, or neutral—with mindfulness. The experience of emotional overload often begins with a moment of rejecting a difficult feeling or emotion.

Modern Western culture expects people to be "happy" all the time and defines this word as feeling upbeat and cheerful—the ubiquitous smiley face. When this form of happiness does not arise, it's common to feel as if something's "wrong" or to experience a sense of inadequacy. It can be highly beneficial to reconsider expectations in this regard. Is this type of happiness always possible? Might happiness be redefined to include a broader range of experiences?

Pleasant, unpleasant, and neutral experiences are always present in our lives. Quite frequently, people don't get what they want, or get what they don't want; or they are separated from those they love and have to deal with people they don't like. On top of this, it's certain that everything we appreciate (including loved ones and ourselves) will change and pass away, and we have no clue when this is going to happen. These are just life's facts, regardless of race, creed, wealth, education level, or power. There's nothing personal in this. If there were a way to get rid of the unpleasant and have only pleasant experiences, inner cultivation and mind training wouldn't make much sense.

Bringing awareness to the experience of events clarifies how temporary these experiences are. The experience of something as overwhelmingly pleasant or unpleasant, for example, ultimately shifts, perhaps losing its intensity, transforming into another feeling, or fading away altogether. Frequently, upon careful observation, that which appeared monumentally or monolithically unpleasant is actually dynamic, with moments of pain interspersed with pleasant or neutral moments.

Experiment: Noticing the Changing Nature of Unpleasant Experience

The following experiment takes only a few minutes, and doesn't require any particular posture or special equipment.

Begin by taking a few deep breaths.

Now turn your attention to any aspect of your experience that is uncomfortable *in this moment.* If you are fortunate enough not to experience any discomfort whatsoever, come back to this experiment later.

If you are able to locate an unpleasant sensation or emotion, take a moment to direct your attention to this experience with as much steadiness, kindness, and curiosity as possible. One common trap in noticing the unpleasant with mindfulness is holding a secret agenda to get rid of the experience by paying attention to it. See if you can just notice it, without trying to change it in any way—not trying to get rid of it, make it stronger, or transform it in any way. Heighten your powers of observation as best you can, noticing the subtle and minute aspects of this experience. What are the sensations in the body like? Do they shift upon observation? Does the intensity change? The location? If the mind begins to sweep you up into the story of the pain, notice "thinking" and gently bring your attention back to the unpleasant experience.

Take a moment to write down what you observed. It might be helpful to refer to this in the future when you are feeling overwhelmed by a similar discomfort.

Notes

_____

When awareness is increased in this way, our overall happiness may increase, too. Another related and useful distinction is between *eudaimonic happiness* and *hedonic pleasure.* Hedonic pleasure is that which derives from external things and events (such as vacations, funny movies, or purchasing that V-neck sweater from Nordstrom!). Eudaimonic happiness is often referred to as human flourishing and points to the deeper kind of happiness that comes from love, generosity, and virtuous deeds. From eudaimonia comes emotional balance and the ability to gracefully accept and adjust to even the most difficult challenges. This is the kind of happiness we're trying to cultivate through the practices offered in this book—a kind of happiness that implies embracing life as a whole and not just a tiny part of it, and one that does not depend on external circumstances.

There's another important reason why mindful awareness results in eudaimonic happiness, and this has to do with insight. It's difficult to uncouple the satisfaction of sense desires from happiness, not simply because of the power of the media, but because of the subtle yet pernicious conflation of two distinct experiences that happen so quickly they usually blend into one experience. As you probably noticed in the exercises above, the desire for something you *don't* have and the desire to get rid of something you *do* have both involve discomfort that can range from mild to acute. In whatever form it arises, from the wisp of a thought about taking your shoes off to obsessive longing for a romantic partner, desire hurts. Two things are happening when you finally obtain the object of your desire: the pain of desire ends and the pleasure of the object is experienced. When the relief of the end of desire is not identified, we believe that the good feeling came completely from attaining the object. To notice the relief that occurs when the pain of desire ends, it generally takes a fairly quiet and concentrated mind that's able to notice desire, tolerate the discomfort of it, and notice what happens to it when it's not immediately acted upon. There's tremendous power and freedom in cultivating this understanding, and we have included several practices in this chapter that will support you in doing this.

Much of great literature has been written about our inability to make this distinction, including Tolstoy's masterpiece *Anna Karenina.* In this novel, Anna is a married aristocrat who falls madly in love with a dashing officer named Alexei Vronsky. Most of the novel's 800plus pages are a cautionary tale about the perils of obsessively pursuing sense pleasures, as unequivocally articulated by Tolstoy in the following quote:

"Vronsky, meanwhile, in spite of the complete realization of what he had so long desired, was not perfectly happy. He soon felt that the realization of his desires gave him no more than a grain of sand out of the mountain of happiness he had expected. It showed him the mistake men make in picturing to themselves happiness as the realization of their desires" (Tolstoy 2008, 1103).

Practice Plan, Week 2

Practice: Breath Awareness and Mindfulness of Feelings

(*recording available at*http://www.newharbinger.com/ 28395)

The practice for this week has the dual purpose of settling the mind through breath awareness and noticing feelings as they arise in a nonjudgmental manner. Both elements of this practice help to heighten awareness and diminish emotional reactivity.

It's common to expect meditation practice to foster "good" feelings. Sometimes it does and sometimes it doesn't. Anxiety or other "negative" emotional experiences can actually increase during meditation. When this occurs, it's helpful to bring awareness to what's happening without trying to push it away or make the meditation "better." Likewise, when meditation does foster a pleasant emotional state, the practice involves bringing awareness to any clinging or grasping to maintain this "positive" feeling. There's no need to feel bad about a meditation practice that doesn't engender peaceful or relaxing feelings. Instead, the meditation practice involves welcoming whatever arises during meditation. Awareness is large enough to hold all emotions, thoughts, and physical sensations.

There's a short Buddhist verse that captures the relationship between the breath and feelings that we'll explore in this practice:

> Feelings come and go
> like clouds in a windy sky.
> Conscious breathing
> is my anchor.

(Nhat Hanh 1997, 8)

We'll use the breath both as an anchor to the present moment and as a way to connect with the spaciousness of awareness. In this way of paying attention, it's possible to observe feelings forming and dissolving without grasping or aversion.

Here's an abridged transcript of the guided meditation recording, for those who prefer to read the instructions first and then practice in silence:

- Find a sitting posture that's upright and alert, yet neither stiff nor rigid. The intention of the practice is to combine alertness, relaxation, and stillness—qualities that aren't typically combined in everyday life. This is a new "gear" for most people, who are accustomed to being either "on" or "off." The position of the body supports the ability of the mind to settle down and sustain nonjudgmental awareness. It helps to have a straight spine, strong in back and tender in the front.

- Allow the hands to rest comfortably, either in your lap or on your thighs, and allow the eyes to gently close. Should this feel uncomfortable for any reason, maintain a soft focus on the floor in front of you.

- Begin with three deep, diaphragmatic breaths.

- After the third exhalation, release the breath to its natural rhythm, letting the belly soften and allowing the breath to flow in and out without manipulation or preference. Gather your attention around the subtle and simple sensations of expansion and contraction in the belly as you breathe.

- Each time you notice the mind wandering from the breath (perhaps remembering something or planning for the future), acknowledge that it has wandered and then gently return the attention to the breath. As best you can, allow this process to occur in a spirit of nonjudging, without giving yourself a hard time. It's not a mistake for the mind to wander, it's just the nature of mind. Upon becoming aware that it has wandered, how gentle and patient can you be in escorting the attention back to the breath?

- Spend ten to fifteen minutes focusing on the breath as the primary object of awareness. Experiment with using a quiet mental label of "rising" on the in-breath and "falling" on the out-breath as a way to steady and stabilize the attention on the breath, while giving the discursive mind the "job" of labeling, paying attention to the sensations of expansion in the belly on the in-breath and deflation or contraction in the belly on the out-breath. This noting technique is very quiet, really like a whisper in the mind. Imagine that 95 percent of your energy and attention is involved in feeling the sensations of the breath in the belly and only 5 percent is used for noting the experience. See if you can allow your attention to ride the waves of the breath, just as a boat rides the waves of the sea.

- For the last five to ten minutes of the meditation, turn your attention toward the feeling tones that accompany every moment of experience. Is this in-breath pleasant, unpleasant, or neutral? When you become aware of judging mind, what is the feeling tone of that experience? You might notice that you are judging yourself for having so many thoughts. How does that judgment feel? Without trying to analyze or create any particular set of experiences, see if you can shift your attention to the subtle and rapidly changing stream of feeling tones that often occur below the threshold of ordinary awareness. Notice, too, any tendencies to cling to the pleasant, zone out on the neutral, or push away the unpleasant.

- Close the meditation with a minute or two of returning the attention to the simple sensations of the breath.

Breath Awareness and Mindfulness of Feelings—FAQs

- "What kind of breathing should I do during the meditation?"

    - After the three initial diaphragmatic breaths, there is no need to create any special type of breathing; just allow the breath to flow naturally.

- "I can't stop my mind from wandering."

    - True! It's nearly impossible to do this. All you need to do, when you notice the mind has wandered, is gently escort it back to the breath.

- "What's the best place in the body to notice the breath?"

    - There are only three places in the body where the breath is easy to follow: the tip of the nostrils and upper lip, the rise and fall of the chest, and the rise and fall of the belly. Choose the place that's easiest for you, and then stick with it, at least for the duration of the meditation. Some people report that focusing on the sensations in the belly is more grounding, especially when there are strong emotions present.

- "Is there a way I am supposed to feel when I meditate?"

  - One of the most problematic misunderstandings that newcomers bring to meditation is the idea that they should be creating a "special" state when they do the practice. Not only is this untrue, but the desire to create calm, or any other idealized mental state, is one of the biggest obstacles to settling into the present moment as it is, which is the heart of these practices.

- "What's the difference between emotions and feeling tones?"

  - The words "emotion" and "feeling" are often used interchangeably in English. For our purposes, however, "emotion" refers to a specific set of responses, as outlined in chapter 2, and "feeling tones" refers to the very quick and simple valence of "pleasant, unpleasant, or neutral" that accompanies every moment of experience.

- "Feeling tones are too quick or too subtle for me to notice them."

  - It actually takes a lot of mindfulness to notice what you can't notice. Good job! Feeling tones can be elusive, and there's no need to worry if you can't identify them. One strategy for tuning in to feeling tones is to intentionally inquire into any strong experience that arises in or out of meditation: is this pleasant, unpleasant, or neutral? These labels are quite powerful, because they interrupt the habitual judgments we hold and invite a more spacious relationship to whatever arises.

Field Observation: Noticing Desire and the End of Desire

See if you can catch desire as it arises, whether *for* something or *to get rid of* something. For the purposes of this exercise, it's helpful to begin with mild feelings, like an itch or the desire for a sweet. See if you can stay with the feeling, noticing the discomfort without either trying to get rid of it or acting on it. See if you can notice when it goes away, and how you feel when it does.

Field Notes

In summary, each moment of experience has a flavor that we're referring to as the "feeling tone." The feeling tone always falls into one of the following three simple categories: pleasant, unpleasant, or neutral. These feeling tones range in intensity from the very subtle pleasant feeling of a wispy fantasy in the mind to the strong unpleasant feeling of intense anger or fear.

Bringing clear, nonjudgmental attention to feeling tones has many possible benefits. First, the feeling tone is the precursor to aversion and clinging, two major culprits in unhappiness and dissatisfaction. Becoming aware of the feeling tone makes it possible to insert a "wedge" of awareness between a subtle response (feeling tone) and an unconscious and often rapid escalation into emotional distress. Second, awareness of feeling tones often reveals their changing nature and thus disabuses us of the distorted perception that this moment of discomfort will last forever. Suicide is perhaps the most tragic consequence of this distorted belief. In becoming aware of feeling tones, we often see that pain—whether physical or emotional—is not a monolithic block of experience, but rather an intricate web of ever-changing experiences that often includes moments of neutrality, or even pleasure.

Paying attention to the ephemeral nature of feeling tones can also bring insight into the truest and deepest sources of happiness—eudaimonic versus hedonic happiness. As we learn to sit with discomfort, a confidence grows in our ability to tolerate unpleasant emotions, and even more importantly, the downward spiral of thoughts and feelings is interrupted.

Chapter 6

Mindfulness of Thoughts

USING YOUR HEAD INSTEAD OF BEING USED BY IT

In the last two chapters, we have explored two important dimensions of experience that are closely related to emotional balance: the body and feeling tones. A third fundamental aspect of the inner landscape that plays a key role in emotional balance is thinking. Despite their invisibility, thoughts are powerful stuff. They have the strength to lead decisions and direct actions. Actually, the way we normally understand the world and ourselves is precisely through the grid of thoughts we superimpose over reality. Our opinions, preconceptions, memories, and expectations, based on previous experience, filter our direct perception and experience in the present. This helps us create a world of experience that is more or less stable and predictable, orienting us to what's happening and facilitating decisions about what to do in a given situation.

A downside of this evolutionarily sophisticated capacity to think is that we have a particular weakness for taking our thoughts at face value, including thoughts that define us or others in ways that lead to suffering. For instance, imagine someone who thinks that he's too old to find a partner (or too young, or too tall or short or fat or thin or intelligent or unintelligent, and so on). This thought will naturally affect his self-confidence and his chances of finding a partner, since self-limiting thoughts often become self-fulfilling prophecies by narrowing perception to only let in information that confirms the belief. Imagine, too, the implications of having fixed ideas about one's children (not only negative thoughts like "My son can't do math," but also positive ones like "My daughter will be a successful lawyer"). Such ideas don't allow the child to be fully seen and accepted as he or she is; instead, the child is perceived through lenses of fear or hope in the adult's mind.

As you might have noticed, we spend much of our adult life thinking. Just as human babies center their identities around their bodies and feelings, we adult humans center our identities in our heads: we see ourselves in terms of what we plan, organize, remember, believe, daydream, anticipate, calculate, comment, evaluate, judge, and so on. Because we spend so much time thinking, it's not surprising that we often end up mistaking our thoughts for reality—confusing the map with the territory, so to speak.

In this chapter, we'll explore how knowing that *you are not your thoughts* is a crucial component of emotional balance. We all have running commentaries in our heads, and they are often mistaken for our true or defining essence. This couldn't be further from the truth, or more the culprit when it comes to emotional distress. But there's a way we can learn to relate to our thoughts—even difficult ones—that nurtures wisdom, spaciousness, and warmth, which in turn fosters emotional balance and resilience. A key aspect of this new way of relating to thoughts involves developing the capacity to recognize thoughts for what they really are—discrete, observable mental events. In this process, the distinction between the thinking mind (the inner chalkboard), thoughts (the things written in chalk), and awareness (the witness of all experience, including the chalkboard) will become clearer. But let's take this walk together, one step at a time.

Thoughts, Emotions, and Moods

At this point, you may be asking yourself the legitimate question: "What does thinking have to do with cultivating emotional balance?" Well, as we'll see, quite a lot. Perhaps you recognize in your own experience how certain thoughts give rise to certain emotions. For example, take a moment and bring to mind someone you love, maybe a dear friend, a child, even a pet. Remember a favorite memory with them, perhaps some time you were having fun together or an experience of deep connection. Go ahead, close your eyes and think about that for a minute or two. Do you notice any change in your emotional state? What about your body? Do you notice any change in your face, your chest, or your belly?

When doing this simple exercise, many people notice a sense of warmth pervading different parts of the body. Perhaps it's an openness in the chest, or maybe the face relaxes a bit. It's also common to experience feelings of love, tenderness, gratitude, and happiness. Just like that, we can evoke different thoughts that will trigger coherent emotional and bodily states. For instance, if you replay in your private theater (your mind) a heated discussion with someone difficult, you may notice that your heart starts racing, your extremities get tense, and your face may even contract a bit. Of course, intentionally elicited memories are somewhat easier to control and tend to provoke less intense emotions compared to thoughts that arise spontaneously, although both can elicit emotions.

Let's do an exercise to see more closely how thoughts and emotions are interrelated.

Exercise: How Would You React?

Imagine the following scenario, and take a few moments to reflect on how you might react:

Yesterday was your birthday, and you have a good friend or a sibling who usually remembers this date and honors it with a call, a beautiful card, or a visit, but this time you didn't hear a word from him.

Keeping this situation in mind, take a moment to think about these questions (and try to resist the temptation to read ahead):

- How would you feel about this?

- What kind of thoughts come to your mind?

- How would you react in this scenario?

- Do these thoughts connect with themes or stories that are familiar in your mind?

Notes

It's amazing how differently people react to this imagined situation. For example, some people would take offense at the apparent slight. Others might assume the person simply forgot and that this happens to everybody sometimes. Others would start worrying about what they might have done to the person that made him "so mad at me that he ignored my birthday." Other people would be concerned about the other person's well-being: "Maybe he was sick or something, so I should call to see if he's okay." Still others might jump to a global evaluation of themselves or their relationships: "Maybe we weren't really close after all," or even "Nobody really cares about me."

These wildly different reactions to an ambiguous situation like this are directly linked to how we perceive and think about the situation. Our overall mood, past experiences, and habitual thoughts are likely to color what we see and how we respond. This means that by opening to new ways of thinking about a particular situation, or even by just giving the person or situation the benefit of the doubt—that is, recognizing the possibility that our thoughts are not the ultimate truth about him or it—it's possible to bring more spaciousness to the situation and change our emotional reactions. This may seem simple, or even obvious, but it's extremely powerful. One misperception can snowball into days of unhappiness.

Now, let's apply this to real life. Bring to mind one current situation that's creating some emotional distress for you. See if there's some way that you're taking things too personally, and see if you can imagine another way to view the same situation, one in which it's not personal. For example, imagine that you weren't acknowledged by your boss for an important achievement at work, or by your spouse for something positive or valuable you did at home, and you feel disappointed and resentful. And then try on the possibility that their lack of acknowledgement isn't personal, that it has nothing to do with you, and that the resentment is extra. Choose an example that works for you and take a few minutes to reflect on what happened, how you interpreted it, and how that made you feel; then explore the possibility of assigning an impersonal explanation to the situation. Do your feelings shift? In the space below, write about any changes you notice, and see if you recognize any patterns of insecurity, self-doubt, or even self-hatred that might give rise to these misperceptions. Sometimes there are irrational beliefs about what you might lose by not taking situations personally (for example, sensitivity toward others, or integrity). Explore this possibility, and then ask yourself if that is really true.

Notes

_____

Thoughts Are Not Reality; Thoughts Are Not You

In Buddhist psychology, the mind is often described as a sixth sense, along with the usual five senses (sight, sound, smell, taste, and touch). From this perspective, just as the eye perceives all kinds of shapes, colors, and lights, the ear perceives all kinds of sounds, and the nose perceive all sorts of smells, the mind perceives all sorts of thoughts: big and small, beautiful and ugly, entertaining and boring, wise and foolish, and so on. Most people wouldn't identify themselves with the colors or shapes they see, or the textures they touch. People don't usually think, for instance, "I am pale green" or "I'm very granular." But thoughts, as objects of the mind, are somewhat different and, perhaps because they're immaterial and internal, we're more apt to mistake them for who we are.

Self-evaluative thoughts are particularly seductive and convincing. They come to mind dressed as ultimate truths. When a thought like "I'm no good," "I'm unlovable," "I've let people down," or "I'm helpless" appears, we soon get completely sucked in and often single these thoughts out from all the other streams of commentary as "words from on high." Though this is not true for everyone, many of us suffer from a deeply habituated tendency to dismiss fantasies and other categories of thought as fanciful fabrications of the mind but take any negative self-judgments as absolute reality. This is exactly why recognizing that thoughts aren't reality can bring tremendous emotional peace.

Depending on the degree of elaboration, thoughts can range from simple, quick bursts of energy in the mind, to discrete thoughts, to elaborate daydreaming. (We owe the distinctions in this diagram to meditation teacher and psychologist Daniel Brown.)

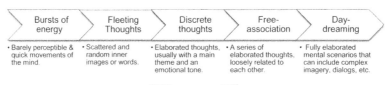

[Figure 3]

Following the diagram above, the closer we are to the left, the more we're able to identify a thought as a thought, and the less likely we are to get lost in that train of thought. The closer we are to the right, the more we tend to get lost in our thoughts and the less aware we are of the fact that we're thinking. It's important to know that there's nothing inherently wrong with free association and daydreaming—actually, those are great capacities of the human mind that can be used in very creative ways. The trouble comes when we're unaware of our thinking process and we imperceptibly climb on board trains of thought that give rise to negative judgments, fear, self-criticism, anger, worry, suspicion, mistrust, and other emotions that sabotage peace of mind and emotional balance.

You may be wondering: "What is the part of me that knows that I'm thinking?" Let's just call it awareness. Though it might seem elusive, the more you get to know it, find your way back to it, and trust it, the happier you'll be. Most of the time, thoughts are just happening without—or beyond—awareness. Mindfulness practice doesn't involve generating thoughts intentionally, controlling your thoughts, or manipulating them. Rather, it involves becoming aware of thoughts *as thoughts,* allowing them to arise and dissipate without holding on to or rejecting them. This capacity to be aware of thoughts can be used *whenever* you remember to pay attention—while meditating or in everyday life. This awareness is not something new that you need to learn. It's already there and available in any moment, no matter what's happening. Awareness is naturally here, but it can go unnoticed for an entire lifetime, so it needs to be explored and known experientially. As you get familiar with your own awareness, you'll come to see how it can become an ultimate refuge, a natural place of balance in the mind and the heart, unlimited in its capacity to meet experience.

Experiment: Recognizing Thoughts as Thoughts

Take a comfortable position and reconnect with your body by straightening your spine, rolling your shoulders back and down, and releasing your belly. Take a couple of deep breaths, releasing all the air from your lungs as you exhale. We'll offer you a few different ways in which you can start playing around with the idea of observing your thoughts as mental events, and noticing them without getting caught in them. You can simply read one suggestion, then close your eyes while you try it on for a minute or two, and then explore the next suggestion. Or you can stay with one of the suggestions if you feel it's particularly useful in helping you to recognize thoughts as thoughts. Remember that you don't need to *try* to think—rest assured that thoughts will come your way! And if they don't for a time, simply enjoy the mental silence.

• Count your thoughts as they arise. It doesn't matter what kind of thought comes through your mind—a memory, an image, an inner comment about this exercise, a plan for tomorrow, and so on. Whatever it is, it will simply count as one thought. Count thoughts from one to ten, and then begin again at one. If you get lost in counting, simply start again at one. If a judgment about not doing it correctly appears, just count that as a thought too, and keep going.

• Visualize yourself sitting on a stream bank, and imagine that the water flowing in front of you is your own mind. Your job is to be aware of the thoughts that flow in the stream. You don't need to catch them, or follow them, or do anything to them. Simply notice them and then watch them go down the current, like leaves floating by.

• Visualize yourself lying in the grass on a lovely clear day. Imagine that your mind is like the vast blue sky above you. Imagine each thought that arises as a cloud formation: some of them will be small, others large; some of them might be puffy and soft, while others will seem dense and heavy. Maybe there are some clouds that cover the sky completely. Still, a cloud is a cloud: it comes and it goes away or vanishes. The task at hand is to see each cloud for what it is.

From your own experience, what did you observe?

Notes

_____

Hopefully it's clear by now that the aim is not to improve thoughts, or to exchange negative thinking for positive thinking. Actually, we're not really big fans of positive thinking as a sustainable path to well-being. What we're encouraging you to do here is to try a *new* way of relating to thoughts that is more spacious and wise. Paradoxically, this will naturally lead to less rumination and more wholesome thoughts, as the thinking process will be free from fixation and drivenness. In this way, you can start using your head instead of being used by it.

Mindfulness, Meditation, and Thoughts

One of the most subtle, yet clear distinctions between meditative mind and everyday mind is whether or not there is awareness of thinking as it occurs. Notice that this in no way implies that thinking should not occur. In fact, the idea of trying to achieve a state where there's no thinking is the single biggest obstacle students face when beginning a meditation practice. Because it's the nature of mind to manufacture thoughts, even the slightest aversion to this natural tendency creates the conditions for dis-ease, struggle, or eventually a downright battle against our own mind—and you guessed it, you will never win in a battle against your mind.

Thoughts not only aren't obstacles in meditation, they're allies. When thoughts appear in meditation, we have the opportunity to explore in exquisite detail how our thinking mind works, to learn which kinds of thoughts have a lot of "grab" in our minds and how it is that we get hooked by them. It's only by *having* thoughts that we can begin to experience the difference between wise thinking and getting lost in thought.

You'll notice that in the recordings that accompany this book, there are never instructions to "get rid of thoughts" or push them away, even slightly. And yet, again and again, people imagine that they hear such instructions, even though they're not actually there. The myth that meditation means having a blissfully empty mind is widespread—and pernicious. Though it is indeed possible for the mind to become profoundly quiet and blissful in meditation, usually the most direct route to a peaceful, collected mind is learning how to neither push unpleasant thoughts away nor cling to pleasant thoughts. This is one of the many paradoxes of contemplative practice.

Just as it's impossible to make the surface of a pond still by smoothing it with your palm, it's not possible to force ourselves into inner silence. Any mental action to calm your mind will only create more ripples in it. Of course, it's hard for the human mind to let things simply be, since it's much more interested in fixing, controlling, improving, and so forth. But to gain emotional balance, it's important to learn to not just do something, but to just sit.

Meditation isn't thinking, but not thinking isn't meditation either. Bringing awareness to the process of thinking and to thoughts as objects of the mind is meditation. Meditation is clear awareness of thinking, which allows us to perceive thoughts as what they actually are—mental events—instead of taking them as something real and solid. By noticing that a thought is a thought, we begin to see the transparency, fluidity, and relativity of thoughts. Softening one's grip on thoughts creates more space in the mind. When we stop getting hooked by thoughts, or lost in them, we can take back the power that we have unconsciously given over to them, and we're in a better position to prevent or overcome emotional imbalance.

When focusing on thoughts during meditation, it doesn't matter if you have thoughts about an intricate blueprint for a mystery novel, the laundry, or the latest drama in a celebrity's life. It doesn't matter if it's a goofy thought, a Nobel Prize – worthy thought, a happy memory, or a plan for your next holiday. When practicing mindfulness of thought, we pay attention to the *contour* of the thought rather than the *content* of it, so to speak. Just as when you practiced mindful breathing it didn't matter if the breath was deep or shallow, long or short, in this practice we're not concerned about the story of the thought—it's simply noticed as a thought.

Thoughts are sneaky objects of meditation. They sometimes pretend they're not thoughts. For instance, during meditation you can have thoughts like "I'm not doing it right," "It's so quiet in here," "I must be one step closer to enlightenment," "This meditation sucks," "I should be doing something more productive,"

"Maybe other types of meditation will work better for my phenotype." A meditation teacher, James Baraz, once said during a retreat, "After twenty years of meditation I notice that I still have just as many judgments as when I started practicing—I just don't believe them anymore." The more you practice, the more frequently, easily, and quickly you're able to notice thoughts as thoughts, even in the course of everyday life. Over time, the volume and intensity of the stream of thoughts running in your head (sometimes called "discursive thinking") actually decreases, leaving more room and energy for insight and creativity. Both decreasing the intensity and frequency of discursive thinking and learning not to believe everything your thoughts say will make you less likely to get stuck in difficult emotions (usually fueled by thoughts) and help you recover faster when you're already in the grip of emotional turmoil.

Practice Plan, Week 3

Meditation Practice: Breath Awareness and Awareness of Thoughts

(*recording available at* http://www.newharbinger.com /28395)

As with previous meditation practices, we encourage you to try this one regularly, every day for a whole week if this is possible, before moving to the next chapter or practice. Taken together, the practices of mindfulness of the body and breath (chapter 4), mindfulness of feelings (chapter 5), and awareness of thoughts (chapter 6) form the basic mindfulness skills that we'll use for the rest of the program to explore specific emotional states. This is why it's important to spend some time with and become familiar with each of these practices.

Here's an abridged transcript of the recording, for those who prefer to read the instructions first and then practice in silence:

- Find a sitting posture that is upright and alert, yet neither stiff nor rigid. The intention of the practice is to combine alertness, relaxation, and stillness—qualities that aren't typically combined in everyday life. The position of the body supports the ability of the mind to settle down and sustain nonjudgmental awareness. It helps to have a straight spine, strong in back and tender in the front.

- Letting the hands rest comfortably, either in your lap or on your thighs, allow the eyes to gently close. Should this feel uncomfortable for any reason, maintain a soft focus on the floor in front of you.

- Begin with three deep, diaphragmatic breaths.

- After the third exhalation, release the breath to its natural rhythm, letting the belly soften and allowing the breath to flow in and out without manipulation or preference. Gather your attention around the subtle and simple sensations of expansion and contraction in the belly as you breathe.

- Practice awareness of breath (ten minutes).

- Each time you notice the mind wandering from the breath (perhaps remembering something or planning for the future), acknowledge that it has wandered and then gently return the attention to the breath. As best you can, allow this process to occur in a spirit of nonjudging, without giving yourself a hard time. It's not a mistake for the mind to wander, it's just the nature of mind. Upon becoming aware that it has wandered, how gentle and patient can you be in escorting the attention back to the breath? There's no need to push thoughts away. Just notice "thinking," and choose to refocus the attention on the breath, allowing the thoughts, or any other distractions that capture attention, to recede naturally on their own. It often helps to remember that thoughts and other "distractions" are as much a part of the meditation as are the moments of nonjudgmental awareness of the breath.

- Practice awareness of thoughts (ten to fifteen minutes).

- As you notice a thought arising, stay with your awareness of the thought, without trying to get rid of it and without allowing yourself to get carried away with the thought. See what happens to your thoughts upon observation. If you find that a thought vanishes upon observation, return attention to the breath.

- It can be helpful to label thoughts as they arise. You might use a general label, such as "thinking," or a more specific one, such as "planning," "judging," or "worrying." For example, the thought "This is really boring" can be labeled as "judging." If choosing specific labels gives rise to more thinking, keep it simple and use the general label, "thinking."

- Each time a thought arises, give it a label, observing what happens to it without analyzing it or letting it carry the mind away. Notice the contour or category of thought, rather than being pulled into the content of the story. As best you can, remain identified with the part of you that's aware of thinking.

- Each time you notice that the mind has become carried away with a thought, return your awareness to the breath and then resume observation of thoughts.

- Thoughts can be very seductive, particularly during sitting meditation. You may find it helpful to think of attention as a spotlight, which can be turned toward the primary object of meditation, whether it's the breath, sound, sensations, or thoughts. This spotlight allows experience to be seen in the clear light of nonjudgmental awareness.

- There's no need to look for thoughts, or to push them away. Using the breath as the primary object of awareness, allow the attention to turn fully toward the thought the moment you become aware of thinking. Then, in addition to labeling the thought, notice what happens next.

- Close the meditation with a minute or two of returning attention to the simple sensations of the breath.

Awareness of Thoughts—FAQs

- "My mind just wouldn't stop thinking."

  - This isn't a problem. Actually, each thought that comes to your mind is an opportunity to practice awareness of thoughts. The amount of discursive thinking will diminish over time, but this is not the goal of the practice. The goal is to simply become aware of thoughts, to see them as thoughts.

- "Sometimes important thoughts come up in this practice, like forgotten memories from my childhood, and I don't know what to do with them."

  - When connecting with awareness, we begin to access resources that weren't as readily available before. Mindfulness is called the practice of insight because it's designed to circumvent discursive thinking, allowing access to a deeper part of the mind. It's not uncommon for deeply buried memories to surface, often accompanied by illuminating insight. Other times, insights arise that are transpersonal—ideas that extend beyond one's personal story or identity, revealing the nature of reality itself. Either way, it's helpful to note the experience without attachment. The insights and important memories have now surfaced, and their value will not be lost to you when you note them without pursuing them or trying to keep them.

- "I started noticing gaps between thoughts. What should I do then?"

  • It's not uncommon that in between thoughts you start noticing gaps in which no thoughts are present. Don't get attached to the gaps of mental silence, and practice simply observing the gaps when there are gaps, just as you practice observing thoughts when there are thoughts.

- "I'm definitely not good at this. I get completely lost in my thoughts every time I practice."

  • Can you see that this, too, is also a thought? If you can, you're doing the practice. Even after years of practice it's common to have meditation sessions when we get fully lost in trains of thoughts. Avoid definitive judgments about your capacity, as these judgments are self-limiting.

When the critic speaks in your mind, you can simply label it as "thought," or even name the critic and say hi to it—"Hi, critic"—and just keep practicing.

- "When I'm labeling thoughts, how specific should the labels be?"

  • Actually, it doesn't matter. You can simply label thoughts as "thinking," or be more specific and use labels like "remembering," "planning," "analyzing," "judging," "worrying," and so on. See what works best for you in terms of recognizing thoughts for what they are: transient, relative, insubstantial, and *not you.*

- "What can I do if a thought arises that creates a strong emotion?"

  • Strong emotions can arise during meditation, and this is a good opportunity to observe firsthand the link between thoughts and emotions. Just as when working with thoughts, observe the emotion without holding on to it or pushing it away, simply noticing how it arises and then slowly dissipates. If the emotion feels too overwhelming, take five to ten deep breaths and practice breath awareness for a few minutes before going back to the main practice.

- "Sometimes I get distracted by having too many instructions in this guided practice."

- People vary in the amount of guidance they need. If there are too many instructions for you, keep it simple. Just read the instructions a couple of times and remember the essential points of the practice. When you know the basic instructions, you can practice without guidance, maybe just setting a timer to sit for a fixed amount of time. (Note: When sitting on our own, we like to use the free app called Insight Timer.)

Practice Log

For each day that you practice the Breath Awareness and Awareness of Thoughts Meditation, fill in the following log. (Download additional copies of the log at http://www.newharbinger.com/28395.) Keeping track of your insights with the practices will help you integrate everything you learn from your experiences over time.

Date and time	What stood out with this practice?

Field Observation: Is It True?

During this week, practice bringing awareness to your thoughts, and observe in particular how different thoughts and thought patterns influence your emotions, your moods, and the way you react or respond to others. Whenever you notice that you're "hooked" by a thought (for instance, a fixed idea or limiting belief about yourself or others, or a strong judgment about a situation), simply ask yourself with openness and curiosity:

- Is this *really* true?

- Am I sure about this?

- Are there other ways to interpret this situation?

- Could there be other angles or additional information that I might be missing?

Practice bringing a healthy dose of skepticism to your thoughts, and see if you can recognize that, no matter how intense a particular thought can be, "This one, too, is a thought."

Field Notes

_____

Thoughts are mental events that we often mistake for solid truths about ourselves and others. Because thoughts are closely related to emotions, learning to recognize that we are not our thoughts contributes significantly to emotional balance.

As we've explored in this chapter, awareness of thoughts (witnessing our thoughts without identifying fully with them) allows us to access alternative ways of understanding any given situation, thus lessening the reactive patterns of attachment, aversion, or avoidance. Although at first it might seem difficult, strange, or even irrelevant, it's perfectly possible to learn to recognize a thought as a thought. The capacity that allows this is called awareness. The relation between awareness and thoughts is analogous to the one between the sky and the clouds. In mindfulness meditation, we learn to identify with awareness (or sky), and become able to recognize thoughts (or clouds) as transient, relative phenomena.

Chapter 7

Exploring Forgiveness

THE KEY TO OPENING THE HEART

One of the important challenges along the path toward emotional balance has to do with the emotional wounds that we carry from our past. If you've made it into adulthood, it's likely that you've suffered your fair share of disappointments, pains, injustices, betrayals, mistreatments, and neglects. Consciously or not, it's equally likely that you've likewise been responsible for *other people's* suffering. For some people these scars might be relatively small—little pebbles—but for many of us these wounds have the heft of boulders that are weighing us down, while at the same time being very hard to let go of. Even if you haven't suffered huge personal traumas, it's likely that you carry relational injuries from the past. Even more broadly, because we're members of the human family, we can also identify with victims of large-scale injustices, such as terrorist attacks, civilian deaths in wars, the brutality of dictatorships, or even the obscene gaps between the rich and the poor that exist in some societies.

In this chapter, we'll be looking at what forgiveness is and how to work with resentment, so that we can begin to heal our relationship with the past and clear space for eudaimonic flourishing. But before delving into what forgiveness is and how to cultivate it, a cautionary note is warranted. In this and in the following chapters, we'll be dealing with topics that can be somewhat challenging, and it's natural that this may raise some resistance. You might feel tempted to stop practicing, skip chapters, or quit the program altogether.

If this happens to you, be assured that it is precisely this willingness to turn toward what is difficult that provides the essential healing aspect of awareness practices. However, this gesture can be as gentle, slow, and gradual as you need. Although no authentic transformation can be forced, all authentic transformation involves effort. Becoming familiar with what is difficult will not only build great inner stability for hard times, but will also help you transform what is difficult into what is meaningful.

What Is Forgiveness?

Forgiveness is the way the heart knows how to heal from the inevitable hurts and disappointments of life. It involves a softening of the heart and a letting go of resentment and anger toward those who have harmed us, betrayed us, or abandoned us (including ourselves!). Granted, it can be really difficult to even think about forgiveness when we feel hurt, and as will become clear, forgiveness shouldn't be rushed or imposed. The heart has its own organic rhythm of opening and closing, which needs to be honored. But one of the beautiful aspects of the human mind and heart is that forgiveness—like other deeply healing states, such as love, compassion, and joy—can be consciously cultivated.

Why might it be important to cultivate forgiveness? Imagine for a moment what the world would look like without forgiveness. Can you imagine living in a world in which every one of the 7.2 billion human beings carried every single hurt, every resentment, accompanied by every anger and desire for revenge? Even from a biological perspective, forgiveness could be seen as a survival strategy for humankind, since without forgiveness our species would have annihilated itself in endless retributions. Thus, forgiveness makes sense not only morally, but also practically.

From time immemorial, wisdom traditions have insisted that forgiveness is the path to attaining enduring peace. In the *Dhammapada,* a collection of sayings of the Buddha, it is said: "In this world hate never yet dispelled hate. Only love dispels hate. This is the law" (I, 5). Closer to our time, and based on a different religious tradition but a similar spiritual insight, Martin Luther King Jr. said: "Violence as a way of achieving racial justice is both impractical and immoral. It is impractical because it is a descending spiral ending in destruction for all. The old law of an eye for an eye leaves everybody blind" (King 1983, 73).

Letting go of resentment and the desire for revenge might be a common definition of forgiveness and, as an idea, it might make a lot of sense. Yet even when the wish is there to release a grudge and open the heart once again, there may still be something standing in the way of forgiveness. Some of these obstacles are deeply held ideas about what forgiveness is and what it isn't.

Before going any further, we would like to invite you to explore your own beliefs about forgiveness.

Exercise

Please write your responses to each question below, taking a moment to reflect on what you truly believe.

1. Who benefits from forgiveness?

_____

2. Is forgiveness the same as reconciliation? If not, what's the difference?

_____

3. Does the act of forgiveness condone or minimize behavior? Why or why not?

_____

4. Is forgiveness a sign of weakness or strength? Why or why not?

_____

5. Does forgiveness require an apology?

_____

6. Is forgiveness a process, or does it happen in a moment? Can it be forced?

_____

7. Does forgiveness always involve forgetting? Please elaborate.

_____

Now we would like to share with you some responses to these questions from others who have suffered greatly and yet have been able to forgive. These are not the "right answers," but simply other perspectives that can both inspire and potentially broaden our own.

Forgiveness Is Freedom from an Inner Prison

Although few would argue that we receive the greatest benefit from the forgiveness we grant to others, we nonetheless act as if forgiveness is a gift we offer to the other person, and remove ourselves from the equation. If we really understood that forgiveness is primarily an act of self-compassion, we would be less inclined to hold on to resentment. Holding on to resentment has been described as swallowing poison and hoping the enemy will die. Although this analogy might seem exaggerated, it points to something important: resentment mainly affects those who feel it, not the object of their resentment. Indeed, the long-term effects of resentment can actually be poisonous to the mind-body.

There's a story about two Tibetan Buddhist monks who meet several years after they had been released from a Chinese prison, where they had been tortured by their jailers. "Have you forgiven them?" asked one monk. The other replied, "Absolutely not! I will never forgive them!" "Well," said the first monk, "I guess they still have you in prison, don't they?" Anger and resentment can feel like the bars of an *inner prison* that quite literally limits our outlook, hinders our imagination, and weakens our self-determination.

When we dwell in resentment, we relinquish our power to those we're angry with. It is said that when the Dalai Lama was asked, "Are you angry at the Chinese?" he replied, "The Chinese have taken everything. Why should I give them my state of mind as well?" The Dalai Lama's response doesn't claim that he's above anger—rather, it's that he chooses to keep the responsibility for his own mind and to work with it, instead of giving up personal power and assuming the identity of a victim. This has nothing to do with being passive in the face of abuse; it simply implies responding from a space of wisdom, rather than just reacting from resentment.

Experiment: Effects of Unforgiveness

Are there times you have been unable to forgive? Reflect on how that choice has affected your life. If holding on to *un* forgiveness was a strategy to achieve something, how has that strategy worked for you?

Forgiveness Is Different from Reconciliation

The distinction between forgiveness and reconciliation is important, and it isn't always apparent. Forgiveness is a process of letting go, not excusing the other person or even reconciling with him. Reconciliation is wonderful when it's possible, but it's not the same as forgiveness.

Reconciliation is more complex because it involves the willingness of both parties to heal and reestablish a relationship that has been damaged. It also requires that the person who committed the fault express authentic remorse and a clear commitment to change his ways.

Forgiveness, instead, is about liberating your own heart and releasing anger and the lust for revenge. Thus, it isn't possible to reconcile without forgiveness, but it's quite possible to forgive without reconciling.

When they're sincere, apologies from the offender are really helpful—when they're insincere, they do more harm than good. But an apology, like reconciliation, is not a prerequisite for forgiveness. Desmond Tutu, who has played a key role in the healing of wounds left by the cruelty and violence of South African apartheid, said, "If the victim could forgive only when the culprit confessed, then the victim would be locked into the culprit's whim, locked into victimhood, whatever her own attitude or intention. That would be palpably unjust" (Tutu 1999, 272).

There are instances where the relationship with the "external" other can't be healed, as when we're dealing with difficult memories of a deceased parent. In these cases, forgiveness can help us heal our relationship with our "internal" other (our memory of the other).

Finally, you can forgive and still opt to never see someone again. None of us need be doomed to live out our days in toxic or abusive relationships. This means that, even if we can't remain on speaking terms with someone, we can still wish the best for them. Don't forget that most of the people against whom we harbor ill will were dear to us at some point, and are now dear to others.

Forgiving Doesn't Minimize or Condone Wrongdoing

A common fear that emerges when we consider forgiving someone is that we might be letting that person off the hook, or that we are sending the message that we're okay with what he or she did, which naturally leads to the scary possibility of repeating a bad story. But in fact, when we forgive we're only letting ourselves off the hook of resentment and anger; what happens with the other person is a whole different story.

When Margaret asked a group of cancer patients if forgiveness condones wrongdoing, she got a very insightful answer: "Intellectually I know it doesn't, but it feels like it does." There's the rub! And sometimes the only way to overcome feelings such as these is to parade them out in the light of day. True forgiveness exposes the awfulness, the abuse, the pain, the hurt, the truth.

Forgiveness does not whitewash, sweep under the carpet, or put a smiley face sticker over injustice. Forgiving does not make an immoral or hurtful act become okay. On the contrary, it says: what happened hurt, but I choose to move on with my life. It's interesting to realize and accept that whether we forgive the other person or not has nothing to do with controlling the other person's intentions, decisions, or actions. People do what they do. What *we* can do is change our relationship with what happened in the past, and set healthy boundaries in the present.

Many of us think forgiving and condoning are the same. However, to condone suggests that the act of wrongdoing is okay, acceptable, even harmless. To forgive, however, is the opposite. Implicit in forgiveness is the reality that harm was caused; otherwise, why even bother to forgive?

Forgiveness Both Requires and Enhances Inner Strength

Often people are clear intellectually that forgiveness isn't a sign of weakness, but still feel like a doormat if they forgive. They also worry that they might be setting themselves up for more suffering. Here it's helpful to distinguish between giving in and forgiving. They sound almost alike and yet are worlds apart. To give in means you don't have the strength or the will to keep fighting. It's like saying "You win." And it can feel like weakness, or at least like you've compromised in some way you didn't really want to. Though you might achieve some degree of resolution, it feels yucky. Forgiveness feels good. If you feel yucky, that's a red flag indicating that something else is going on.

In an interview in 1931, Mohandas Gandhi was asked if he didn't find it unwise to forgive Britain, which had been guilty of so many deaths in India, to which he responded: "I do not know a single instance where forgiveness has been found so wanting as to be impolitic ... The weak can never forgive. Forgiveness is an attribute of the strong" (Gandhi 2000, 302). Similarly, the *Bhagavad Gita* also underscores the relationship between strength and forgiveness: "If you want to see the heroic, look at those who can love in return for hatred. If you want to see the brave, look for those who can forgive." If you think about it, the idea that angry and vengeful characters are heroic and courageous only works in Hollywood. It requires a fair amount of character strength to be able to forgive and to take a nonviolent stance instead of reacting with a knee-jerk reflex of punching back.

Forgiveness Is a Process That Can't Be Forced

You don't have to forgive for good. This is the really good news. You can put your toes in the soothing waters of forgiveness and go right back to the parched but familiar landscape of unforgiveness, if you need to. Some things take time to work through and this depends on many factors—especially on how seriously you were hurt.

Forgiveness can be cultivated, but it can't be forced. A garden is a good metaphor for this process. You can't force a plant to bloom or bear fruit, no matter how carefully you've tended it. At the same time, if you don't plant the seeds and water and feed the garden, there will be no flowers. Though the seasons of the heart are often unfathomable to the mind, they nonetheless follow their own laws, just like the cycles of nature. Loss and suffering are inevitable, and the heart has its own ways of facing these challenges. Grief may be blatant and recognizable, or it might be at work deep within for a long time, and it only takes a moment of practice or insight for the heart to let go.

It's also important to keep in mind that the process of forgiveness is not a simple and linear one. As you keep doing the awareness practices you will become better able to disidentify with the feelings of anger and resentment, and also with the mental discourses that keep you locked in victimhood. However, it's likely that time and time again the mind will be clouded with strong emotions and thoughts; after all, they've been habituated countless times. The key here is patience and consistency. Like a good gardener, just keep pulling out the grudges and watering forgiveness in your inner garden.

Overcoming Resentment Doesn't Imply Forgetting

The misunderstanding that forgiving means forgetting seems to be at the root of many tragic dramas. Ongoing struggles in the world are due in large part to the fear that to forgive a wrong done to others is to be disloyal to their suffering. We all know of stories where family members haven't spoken in decades.

Often, no one can remember what the original fight was about, yet the sides have been drawn and to cross them is to be disloyal. Vendettas are handed down from generation to generation. There can even be fear of disloyalty to *our own* suffering, as captured beautifully in a quote attributed to the great Sufi teacher Hazrat Inayat Khan: "Don't be concerned about being disloyal to your pain by being joyous."

But forgiveness is not forgetting. Forgiveness is how you hold in your heart something that is wrong while you take the necessary steps to correct it and to help prevent it from happening again. Thankfully, we have great examples of people who have walked this path before us, not only surviving terrible injustice and violence toward themselves or loved ones, but also showing us how forgiveness can transform the deepest pain of senseless violence into love and meaning in the service of others.

Immaculée Ilibagiza is a Tutsi who survived the genocide in Rwanda because a Hutu pastor hid her, along with seven other women, in a tiny bathroom in his home for ninety-one days. In her book, *Left to Tell* (Ilibagiza 2006), she describes the nightmare of hiding in this tiny space while she heard bloodthirsty Hutus outside the window, promising to hunt her down and kill her. Everyone in her family was killed except for one brother who was studying in Senegal at the time. Ilibagiza called on her faith to find the strength to forgive those who murdered her family and became an important voice in breaking the cycle of violence in Rwanda.

Another modern forgiveness hero is Izzeldin Abuelaish. Abuelaish is a Palestinian physician with a master's degree in public health from Harvard. He was also the first Palestinian doctor to receive a staff position at an Israeli hospital. Three of his daughters were killed in their home by Israeli tank fire during the Gaza War of 2008–2009. He chose to forgive the murder of his children—a possibility almost inconceivable for most parents to even contemplate. Two years later he wrote a book, *I Shall Not Hate: A Gaza Doctor's Journey on the Road to Peace and Human Dignity* (2011), and founded the Daughters for Life Foundation in memory of his three daughters. The mission of the foundation is to "advance the education and health of girls and women in the Middle East. We believe that lasting peace in the Middle East depends on empowering girls and young women through education to develop strong voices for the betterment of life throughout the Middle East" (http://www.daughtersforlife.com).

These are just two stories among countless others that can inspire us to transform our pain into meaningful action through the power of forgiveness. Almost anywhere where horror is present in human history, the strength and wisdom of the human spirit is also shining.

Four Steps to Forgiveness

You might be thinking, *Okay, I'm ready to try it. How do I do it?* Many people are willing to try to forgive, but just don't know how to do it. Here are four simple steps that can open the doors of the heart to ease and freedom. The first three involve reflection and becoming familiar with a particular perspective. The fourth step is the meditative practice itself, which can be done both formally and informally, for as long and as often as you like. It's helpful to think of forgiveness as a skill that can be improved and enlarged with practice, just like playing the piano.

Step 1: Recognize that suffering exists. Whatever your difficulties, you're not alone. There is no plot against you, and your suffering isn't your fault. Accept the fact that, as much as others have hurt you, you have also been the agent of suffering. We are all fallible and we will hurt and be hurt by others, especially the ones we love; therefore forgiveness is not optional but necessary if we live and interact with others. Difficulties, misunderstandings, and offenses are simply a part of the human condition. We can do our best to reduce them, but we can't get rid of them.

Step 2: Imagine the other person's perspective. The more we can see our enemies as human beings, just like us, the harder it is to condemn them. Notice any resistance that comes when you imagine the suffering of those who have harmed you. This is common and can quickly harden into habit, and we shouldn't mistake what is habitual for what is natural. Underneath the habit of reducing our enemies to one-dimensional bad guy cartoons is the capacity of the human heart to feel compassion for everyone. Henry Wadsworth Longfellow wrote: "If we could read the secret history of our enemies, we should find in each man's life sorrow and suffering enough to disarm all hostility" (Longfellow 2000, 797). According to different contemplative traditions, hostility itself is an expression of suffering, and in the framework of Nonviolent Communication (Rosenberg 2003), unskillful behaviors are seen as "tragic expressions of unmet needs" (see chapter 11). Intuiting the needs and suffering behind the annoying and painful actions of others involves cultivating our moral imagination, stepping into other people's shoes, and looking at the world from their perspective, which is often both humbling and heart-opening.

Step 3: Look at the consequences for yourself and others. What are the consequences that you are experiencing right now—in your body, in your mind, in your energy, in your thoughts, in your relationships—while in the state of *un* forgiveness? What would be the consequences of forgiving?

What might you and others gain or lose? Because of the relationship between unforgiveness and physical and psychological illness, forgiveness research has increased exponentially in the last fifteen years. Forgiveness has been associated with reduced stress and reduced anger (Harris et al. 2006), reduced depression, anxiety, and cholesterol levels (Friedberg, Suchday, and Srinivas 2009), better sleep (Stoia-Caraballo et al. 2008), and reduced back pain (Carson et al. 2005), to name just a few findings. Could unforgiveness be linked to these difficulties, or others, in your own life?

Step 4: Practice forgiveness meditation. Forgiveness, like happiness, is a skill that can be practiced and learned. You don't need to wait for grace or inspiration to strike. Included in this chapter is a guided meditation on forgiveness. Try working with it for at least one week and see what happens. Sometimes people find that, even if the heart is feeling closed and dry, practicing forgiveness and inclining the mind in its direction each day noticeably improves their quality of life.

Practice Plan, Week 4

Meditation Practice: Forgiveness

(*recording available at* http://www.newharbinger.com /28395)

For the following guided forgiveness meditation, please find a comfortable sitting position, in a place that's quiet and undisturbed, and in a posture that supports both ease and alertness. You can do this practice by reading the instructions below and following each step, or simply by following the guided instructions on the recording.

It might be helpful, before we begin, to remember that the heart has its own natural rhythms of opening and closing. As you work with this practice, you'll notice differences from day to day. But although forgiveness can't be forced, it *can* be encouraged. The first step is always to honor what's here, in this moment. It can also help to remember that forgiveness does not excuse, condone, or justify harmful actions. Nor does it require you to reconcile with, seek out, or even speak to the person who has harmed you. It's quite simply a movement of the heart, this capacity in all of our hearts to self-heal by first acknowledging the pain and then choosing to let go, refusing to allow the heart to harden from bitterness and resentment.

- Begin with three deep, diaphragmatic breaths, allowing each in-breath and out-breath to soothe the nervous system and to bring your awareness into the present moment. After the third exhalation, let the breath find its own natural rhythm again, just as it does when you're not manipulating it.

- Gently focus your attention on the chest area as you breathe, feeling any sensations associated with the rising and falling of the breath as it moves in and out of this area. See if you can find the "heart center"—that tender spot right in the center of the chest that's pierced by strong feelings of love or sorrow—and see if you can imagine breathing in and out of this tender place. And now, check in to see how you feel in this moment ... right in the center of your chest ... what's there? Are there feelings of tightness or quivering? Or maybe just a blank kind of numbness? Perhaps you feel softness, sensitivity, or openness?

• Take a moment to breathe gently into the center of your heart, and notice any barriers you might have erected or emotions you've been carrying because you *haven't* forgiven yourself or others. Allow yourself to feel the pain of keeping your heart closed. Feel into the places in the heart that have *not* forgiven.

Forgiveness from Others

• Now, breathing softly, let yourself remember and visualize the ways you may have hurt others. It's usually most effective to begin with the small things, and to bring to mind only that which you can meet with kindness and equanimity. As best you can, let yourself bear witness to the pain you have caused out of your own fear and confusion, feeling any sorrow or regret that might arise as you do this and holding the pain of the situation—theirs *and* yours—with as much tenderness as you can. Sense the possibility of finally releasing these burdens by asking for forgiveness. Take as much time as you need to picture each memory, each situation, that still weighs on your heart. And then, as each person comes to mind, gently repeat:

"For any way I've hurt or harmed you, I ask for your forgiveness. I ask for your forgiveness."

- Let yourself remember and feel the fear, pain, anger, or confusion that led you to hurt this person and then silently continue with asking for forgiveness.

- Looking through "the eyes of the heart," see how these hurtful actions were "tragic expressions of your own unmet needs." Perhaps the need to be loved or respected, or the need for safety or peace. And notice how the fact that we hurt others as much as they hurt us just makes us part of the human family. Allow yourself to feel moved by the poignancy of this dilemma—by how we all fall short of our ideals and often don't know *what* we're needing, let alone how to get our needs met.

Self-Forgiveness

- Now take a moment to feel your own precious body and life. Feel the breath, breathing you into existence moment by moment, and the miracle of your body, your heart, and your mind.

- Bring to mind any ways you might have hurt or harmed yourself. We can be experts at self-sabotage. See if you can bring the same honest but tender awareness to the ways you've inflicted suffering on yourself, whether through self-criticism, overeating, or other physical harm. As you picture these scenarios, allow your heart to be penetrated, to be moved by the poignancy of these expressions of self-betrayal or self-abandonment. Feel the sorrow you've carried, and sense the possibility of releasing these burdens. Extend forgiveness for each act of harm, one by one, repeating to yourself:

"For any ways I've hurt myself through action or inaction, out of my own fear, pain, and confusion, I now extend heartfelt forgiveness ... I forgive myself. I forgive myself."

How does it feel, just in this moment, to offer yourself the gift of forgiveness?

Forgiveness for Others

- And now, bring to mind those who may have hurt or harmed *you.* Here, it's *especially* important to begin with the smaller hurts, not the most difficult ones. Feel the sorrow you've carried from the past. Can you touch a place in your heart that longs to be free of this burden? There are *so* many ways we've all been harmed by others—abused or abandoned, knowingly or unknowingly, in thought, word, or deed. As you recall each incident, remember that each person, too, has caused suffering out of his or her own fear, blindness, and sorrow.

- Now sense that you can release this burden of pain by gradually extending forgiveness as your heart is ready, letting the images and feelings arise and be met with tenderness. Reciting to yourself, but never forcing:

> "I've carried this pain in my heart long enough. To the extent that I'm ready, I offer you forgiveness."

- Remember that forgiveness neither condones nor minimizes wrongdoing. If the action was not wrong to begin with, it would not require forgiveness. Remember also that you can forgive in this moment and return to nonforgiveness if you need to. Or you might forgive and discover a deeper layer of sadness or anger waiting to be felt, known, and met with mindfulness. True forgiveness asks that we feel it all; by actually feeling the pain and hurt, it becomes possible to let go and move on. Try again to "dip your toes" into the cool waters of forgiveness, even if you choose to take them right out again. In the next few minutes, continue remembering ways you've been hurt, and see if the heart is willing to let go. "I forgive you ... I forgive you..."

- In the last minute or two of this practice, bring your attention back to the sensations in the heart center as you breathe, and see if you can imbue each in-breath with kindness and each out-breath with ease. Breathing in kindness, breathing out ease.

- Close your practice with a moment of rejoicing in your courage and commitment to live openheartedly. May this be of benefit to you, and to everyone around you.

Practice Log

For each day that you did the meditation on forgiveness, fill in the following log—which you can download additional copies of at http://www.newharb inger.com/28395. Keeping track of your insights with the practices will help you integrate what you learn from your experiences over time. track of your insights with the practices will help you integrate what you learn from your experiences over time.

Date and time	What stood out with this practice?

Field Observation: Everyday Forgiveness

"Season" each day of the coming week with moments of forgiveness. Can you approach your days with a willingness to start fresh and to not carry resentment or grudges? Whenever possible, write brief daily notes about how this attitude affects your day and your interactions.

Field Notes

_____

Although forgiveness can't be forced or hurried, it's definitely possible to cultivate a mindset in which forgiveness can arise. Forgiveness is a process of softening the heart and letting go of resentment, and since it's an organic process, it's only natural that it takes some time and effort until it spontaneously blossoms. When practice gets rough, remember that forgiveness doesn't let others off the hook or make an immoral or hurtful act become okay. On the contrary, forgiveness involves recognizing that what happened hurt, yet choosing to move on with one's life. Forgiveness is an empowering act by which you declare your freedom from the tyranny of resentment.

Finally, remember that forgiving yourself is at least as important as forgiving others. In fact, both aspects are intimately linked. The main practice, then, consists of expanding our mind-heart to understand our own and other people's shortcomings as part of our shared human condition. We can still work to heal the hurt and prevent future suffering, while at the same time choosing not to leave any part of humanity, and any part of ourselves, outside our circle of care.

Deep bows and gratitude to Jack Kornfield and Fred Luskin for their insights and inspiration on the topic of forgiveness. Please see "Additional Resources" for their books on this topic.

Chapter 8

Working with Anger

COSTLY FUEL THAT BURNS HOT!

The mindfulness practices that you have been learning in the previous three chapters are designed to build important inner resources for your journey along the path to cultivating emotional balance, particularly when dealing with difficult emotions. First, training your mind to be in the present moment with an open and nonreactive attitude sharpens your capacity to pay attention, and this is the tool that allows you to be aware of emotional experiences as they manifest in the mind and body. Just as people who begin a yoga practice might feel parts of their bodies they had no idea even existed, you may recognize in your own experience that the mindfulness practices are helping you become better able to perceive physical sensations, thoughts, and emotional patterns that used to go unnoticed.

This heightened awareness is crucial for exploring and healing difficult emotions, precisely because we humans tend to avoid what is unpleasant. Psychologists call this strategy "experiential avoidance," and it's associated with all sorts of emotional problems, particularly anxiety and depression. The good news is that we also know that mindfulness practice diminishes experiential avoidance, and this might be one reason why mindfulness is effective in decreasing emotional distress and enhancing psychological well-being.

Besides increasing and sharpening awareness, mindfulness practice also provides a stable and capacious inner space from which to explore more challenging inner landscapes. In the same way that young children need a safe relationship with their caretakers to feel confident enough to explore new environments—which is called "secure attachment"—we adults need to develop a safe relationship with ourselves in order to explore difficult emotions. Mindfulness practice provides a stable ground of warm equanimity that results from parenting ourselves both on and off the meditation cushion.

We can also think of mindfulness as a safe base camp where we can return and recover from our expeditions to the deep caves of difficult emotions such as anger (this chapter) and fear (chapter 10). Interestingly, this inner base camp also helps us unhook from getting overly attached to positive experiences when we go on expeditions to the high peaks of pleasant emotions such as joy, gratitude, love, and compassion. These emotions are lovely, and deserve to be fully felt and known. They become problematic, however, when we try to hold on to them, wasting energy and the precious present moment on that which has now become the past.

What Is Anger?

Anger is a universal emotion whose main adaptive function is to remove obstacles that thwart us. When we feel anger, it's because the primitive brain is trying to tell us that something needs to change (for example, that we need to remove something that's blocking us). We share this emotion with other mammals and even with reptiles. Baby humans come already well equipped with the capacity to get angry. You will see this if you hold a baby by her arms from behind, preventing her from grabbing an appealing toy that is in front of her—she will get pretty angry, furrowing her brow, tightening her muscles, trying to move forcefully to get the toy, and perhaps shouting with a squeaky voice. When the baby grows up, she can have an analogous reaction when someone cuts her off on the road, especially if she's already late for an important meeting! Anger also shows up when you—or others you feel connected to—are treated unjustly, or when someone or something prevents you from meeting your goals and needs.

Although it's quite possible to get mad at ourselves (we'll explore this when we talk about self-compassion in chapter 11), the energy of anger is generally directed outward and it's often linked with blame. This tendency to blame, strike out, punish, and retaliate makes anger a particularly challenging emotion to sit with, and a big source of interpersonal suffering. When we feel anger toward someone, our sense of "self" and "other" tends to solidify in the mind. In this state, we tend to exaggerate all the negative qualities of the other person and become blind to his positive attributes, which in turn feeds the aversion. In our minds, the complexity and nuance of the other is reduced to a monolithic negative cartoon called "the enemy."

We often wonder why we're angriest at those we're closest to. For one thing, people who know us intimately also know what can hurt us the most. Someone once said, "Your family knows how to push your buttons because they actually installed them." But a less glib reason is that it tends to be safer to show anger to an intimate than to a stranger. Sometimes you can express aggression to your partner when you're actually mad at your boss ... because it's less likely (although not impossible) that your partner will fire you. In fact, we can be frustrated about ourselves but direct our anger outside, and it's quite fascinating that we can even get angry at inanimate objects—a door, a table, a wall, or a shoe. This reveals something interesting: although it feels as if the source of anger is out there, the fact is that anger comes from within. Other people are just pretending to be the real enemies, while they actually are our "patience coaches," offering us opportunities to explore and tame the anger habit. If everyone was nice and considerate, how could we train in patience?

There's an interesting old story about a man who was sailing his boat. The day had started clear and sunny, but after a while a dense fog rolled in. As the man decided to go back to the shore, he noticed the profile of another boat coming in his direction. "Keep your distance!" the boatman shouted, concerned about a possible collision. However, the other boat kept approaching. The boatman used all his skills to swiftly shift the direction of his boat, so that there was even more room for the other boat. He got really upset when he saw that the other boat changed its own course, now coming directly to him. "Stay out of my way!" he shouted again, but the other boat just kept coming closer, until it finally crashed into his boat.

The man was enraged: "You idiot! What the hell are you doing?!" He got totally worked up and continued his rampage until the fog lifted enough so that he was able to see that the other boat was empty—it was just an old abandoned boat floating downstream. He was quite perplexed: To whom could he express his anger? Could he project his anger onto an empty boat? Without a person to blame, it was impossible to keep the story of anger going.

Bringing this story a step closer to our own experience, we can ask ourselves: Do we ever get mad at "empty boats"? If so, where does this anger come from? Where does it go?

Becoming aware of the inner terrain of anger can be very helpful in catching it sooner and sparing ourselves and others the hurt and regret that often ensue from acting out of anger. To work with anger, we need to see the space between trigger and reaction in order to mindfully look within. Try the following experiment.

Experiment: Exploring Anger Triggers and Reactions

What triggers your anger? Make a list of your hottest triggers.

_____

How do you usually react when you're angry? List your "Top Five" anger reactions.

_____

Do you notice patterns or themes in your responses?

_____

Door Number Four

Anger is tricky because there's a cost both to showing anger and to suppressing it. Suppressing it doesn't actually solve anything. It only postpones having to deal with anger, while the anger itself keeps quietly simmering under the surface, wreaking havoc with our bodies. But if we show it, almost invariably we either hurt others or provoke retaliation. Another common habit is unconsciously "feeding" the mind states of anger with our stories of blame and victimization, thereby reinforcing the anger habit.

It's rare that therapists nowadays advise their clients to act out their anger with real or symbolic others (punching pillows, shouting loudly in an empty room, and so on), partially because brain science has demonstrated that each time anger is expressed it gets rehearsed and strengthened. The idea that if you let your anger out you will reach peace and calm is simply not true—the satisfaction of the discharge will invariably be a very transient relief, and anger will come back again. Tibetan meditation teacher Chögyam Trungpa said about this self-reinforcing cycle: "You cannot really eliminate pain through aggression. The more you kill, the more you strengthen the killer who will create new things to be killed. The aggression grows until finally there is no space; the whole environment has been solidified" (Trungpa 1999, 73).

Most of us know that we can actually get a certain satisfaction or relief when we express aggression. There can be a seductive quality to expressing anger, and an adrenaline rush, and that's why it can become a habit, even an addiction. In fact, anger is like a fuel. When we get angry, we can feel energized, stronger, and bigger—picture an angry cat with a curved spine and raised hackles, pretending to be bigger than it is to scare away what it's actually afraid of. However, anger isn't a very efficient fuel, because it burns hot and costly. It can be quite polluting on the inside and outside, and it's heavy and corrosive to the system. Moreover, as the boatman story suggests, the first and main recipient of anger is the angry person—you are the primary recipient of your own anger. There is a beautifully simple Confucian proverb that capures this: "When you embark on a journey of revenge, dig two graves."

Fortunately, there are other options besides the "three doors" of suppression, expression, and unconscious fueling. When insults or obstacles are perceived, it's normal for an anger response to arise. It's just our nature and evolutionary history at work. Though we may succeed in becoming angry less often, anger will always be a part of our emotional lives; it is therefore critical to learn how to relate skillfully with this challenging energy. As soon as you remember that you're not just a victim of your anger, that you can actually use it as a path of self-discovery to develop mindfulness, you can begin to practice being present with the feeling of anger, connecting with it, and allowing its energy to arise and pass away without acting on it or suppressing it. This is "door number four." Don't underestimate the power of this simple method. Like much of meditation, it's simple but not easy.

The capacity to work with anger mindfully is not a binary proposition, something you either have or don't. It's a practice that builds gradually, strengthening the muscle of mindfulness in the face of pleasant *and* unpleasant experiences. Instead of identifying with, rejecting, or being unaware of anger, we can learn to approach it with openness and curiosity, trusting that anger has something to teach us, and that this can be a very productive part of practice. This might not be a self-evident idea, but it's a very important one to get right: anger is not outside of mindfulness practice. It actually provides you with an exceptional opportunity to practice; to open up when habit tells you to shut down, to connect with experience when habit makes you disconnect, and to question if the image you've constructed of yourself and others is as solid as it appears.

Exercise: Mindfulness of Anger

This is a guided visualization exercise in which you will remember a time when you were angry in order to chart the "inner geography" of anger. By encouraging us to notice where sensations show up in the body, the quality of those sensations, and how they change, this exercise helps us become familiar with and befriend this challenging form of energy and recognize it more readily when it arises. Try not to do this exercise in a rush. Allow enough space before and after the main part of the exercise to be able to practice mindfulness of breathing. The intention here is not to end up with aroused anger, but to experience anger in a safe way, watching the sensations change in the body.

Use the following instructions as a guide, modifying them as needed. Please read each bullet point and then take two to three minutes to follow the instructions before moving to the next bullet. Remember that you are in full control of this exercise. You can adapt the instructions and regulate their intensity as much as you want.

• Sit in meditation posture, in a comfortable yet alert position, with your hands resting comfortably and your eyes gently closed. Check in with your body, feeling the places where it makes contact with the chair or floor.

• Take some deep breaths, completely filling the torso with air, then completely releasing the breath.

• Think back to a time when you experienced anger. It could be this year or last, but should be relatively recent. You don't need to choose your worst anger episode—actually, it's wise to start with something smaller—but it has to be something that feels real. Envision and experience what happened, allowing yourself to feel the anger again, right now. Allow the feeling to get as strong as possible within your safe zone.

• Often, other emotions arise when remembering an angry episode, such as sadness or fear. For now, see if you can stay with the feeling of anger.

• Where in your body do you experience anger? Explore this feeling. You may be tempted to try to push it away. Instead, investigate how it feels in the body, noticing gross and subtle sensations throughout the field of physical sensation. Does the sensation increase or decrease in intensity as you notice it? Does it change or move? Does it have a quality of warmth or coolness?

• Practice bringing compassion to the anger. This feeling is normal, part of being human; we all experience it at times. See if you can cradle your own anger like a mother cradling her precious newborn child. What happens as you hold it in this way, with tenderness and care?

• And now, say goodbye to this feeling. Slowly bring your attention back to your breath and stay with it for a while, letting your emotions settle into the spaciousness of your breath and awareness.

After you finish, reflect on the following questions: Which sensations did you notice in your body? Did the sensations change as you observed them? Were you able to bring compassion to the anger? How did you do that? What happened to the anger when you did this?

Notes

_____

Anger Profiles

An important part of working with anger mindfully involves becoming familiar with the way anger manifests in your life. Although anger is a basic and universal emotion, we all have different "anger profiles" (Ekman 2003) based on three factors:

- Onset: How long does it take for you to get angry?

- Intensity: How high does your anger go?

- Cooldown: How long does it take for you to get over it?

Look at the following graphs:

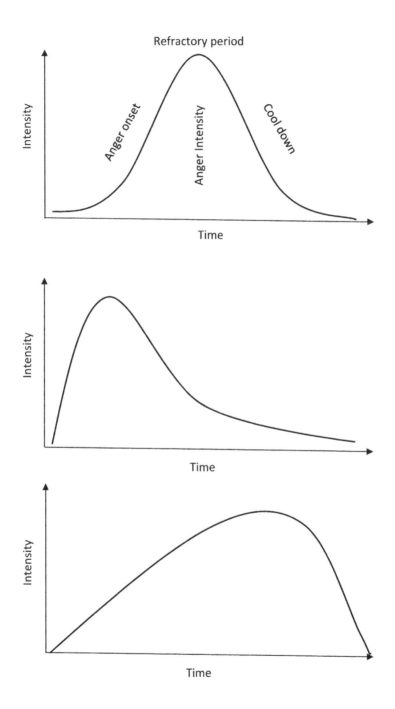

Some people can get angry in the blink of an eye, while for others anger is an emotion that builds up over the course of many hours. While some people typically experience rather mild forms of anger, such as irritation or annoyance, others can get enraged or furious at the slightest provocation. For some, it's easy to cool down and move on to the next thing, while others ruminate about what made them angry for days. Based on these factors, we can reflect on our own anger profiles and observe whether these profiles change when we work mindfully with anger. We can also reflect on the anger profiles of people we are close to, which will allow us to become more skillful in dealing with their anger.

When anger is experienced, it can be difficult or even impossible to think clearly, especially if the anger is very intense. This is the "refractory period" (Ekman 2003). In this phase, we react swiftly and unconsciously, often behaving in ways that are not typical for us. We might feel as if we're "blinded by anger" or have "lost our minds" in anger. The refractory period lasts from the time the flame ignites until it begins to cool down, and it applies to any emotion, not just anger. During that time, it's like we're wearing colored glasses that cause us to see everything through the lens of that particular emotion.

Remembering this, we're more likely to give ourselves and others space to cool down and let the refractory period pass before trying to resolve an issue. When we're in the grip of anger, it's hard to see the big picture, and to take in feedback. Sometimes people become angry because of a lack of a sense of control over their own lives, and telling them what to do only fuels this tension.

When we're angry, particularly in this intense refractory period, we see and believe only that which confirms our anger. For example, if we feel angry at the telephone company for making an error on our bill, we might remember all the other times we've had problems with phone companies, rather than recalling all the times that our phone service and bills have been problem-free. These cognitive distortions help perpetuate anger, making it harder for the mind to see other perspectives.

Experiment: Draw Your Anger Profile

Reflect on times you've gotten angry, and graph your typical anger response (onset, intensity, duration, and cooldown). If you feel that your anger responses are too varied for a single profile, work with an "average" line. As you do this, try to be as objective as you can, like a meteorologist describing weather patterns.

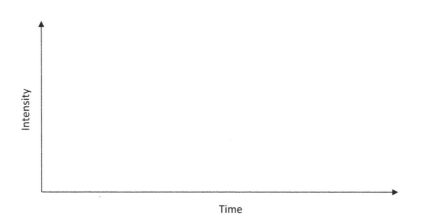

Looking at your graph:

- What do you notice?

- Considering the shape of your graph, what could be helpful in terms of taking care of your anger in a way that decreases suffering in yourself and others? For example, if your anger has a steep onset, you might benefit from the practice of asking yourself, "Am I sure about this?" and trying to gather more information about the situation that is triggering your anger. Perhaps it would be helpful to share this information with those closest to you, so they can support you in responding more skillfully, or not take your reactions as personally.

Notes

_____

If you find this experiment helpful, you might try the interactive version, "Charting Your Anger Profile," available at http://www.paulekman.com. This tool allows you to further explore your profile by adding more characteristics, and gives you the opportunity to compare your profile with that of an intimate partner. your profile by adding more characteristics, and gives you the opportunity to compare your profile with that of an intimate partner.

Practice Plan, Week 5

Meditation Practice: Mindfulness of Breath, Thoughts, and Mental States

(*recording available at* http://www.newharbinger.com
 /28395)

For this guided meditation, we'll begin with awareness of the breath, expand the field of awareness to include thoughts and sensations, and then add instructions for bringing mindfulness to mental states and emotions.

Allow the body to settle into a posture that supports the qualities of stillness, alertness, and relaxation. For most people, this can be accomplished by sitting in a chair in a way that embodies dignity without tension. Take a moment to find a feeling of uprightness in the spine, while at the same time relaxing the muscles in the face, neck, and shoulders.

Begin with three deep, diaphragmatic breaths, allowing the out-breath to be even longer than the in-breath.

After your third out-breath, let the breath find its own natural pace, relinquishing any control of the breath.

Gently begin to gather your attention on the sensations in the belly as you breathe.

As you direct your attention to the breath, see if you can bring kindness, patience, and humor to the wandering mind, especially at the beginning of the meditation practice.

See if you can savor the experience of the breath as you might savor a gourmet meal—each bite, each breath, unique and delicious.

Maintaining the breath as an anchor or home base for your attention, expand the field of awareness to include thoughts as objects of attention.

Whenever you become aware of thinking, use a quiet label of "thinking," or more specific labels such as "planning" or "judging," and see if you can maintain awareness of the thought without either trying to get rid of it or getting lost in the story of the thought. Whether it's a vague wisp of a thought, or a strong story line, simply note "thinking, thinking."

If the thought fades or vanishes, return your attention to the breath.

If a sensation or a sound becomes strong enough to call your attention away from the breath, allow *it* to become the new primary object of your awareness, exploring the experience with steady, kind curiosity—and without any agenda to change or get rid of it.

You might also notice the feeling tone—pleasant, unpleasant, or neutral—since feeling tones tend to be more apparent with sounds and sensations.

Let the breath continue to be your anchor or home base, returning your attention to the sensations of the in-breath and the out-breath when thoughts and sensations aren't strong enough to call your attention away, and using a soft mental label to note and acknowledge thoughts, sounds, sensations, and the breath.

Now, expand your field of awareness even further to include emotions and mental states. These can be challenging to attend to mindfully because they can be both very subtle and very strong.

Emotions like anger or anxiety can be strong and uncomfortable, making it hard to sit still and be present for them. There are several ways to make this easier. First, rather than pursuing the story in the mind, notice the physical sensations that accompany that emotion. See if you can track the inner geography of anger or fear.

It can also be helpful to find an accurate label. There are many flavors of anger, such as irritation, annoyance, rage, resentment, or aggravation. Finding the right label can give you the same feeling as hitting a tennis ball on the sweet spot of your racket—it clicks.

Sometimes emotions can feel threatening and there's a fear that they might swallow us up or overwhelm us. As real as this threat might feel, it's usually irrational. You might experiment with saying to yourself something like, "Okay, let me die of boredom, or restlessness, or even frustration," and then see what happens next.

For both strong and subtle emotions, it can also be helpful to give yourself permission to "peek behind the curtain" for a moment to see what you're feeling. You don't have to stay long, or dig anything up. So, right now, just take a quick peek—perhaps feeling right into the center of your chest—giving yourself permission to return to the breath whenever you need to.

For the remainder of the meditation, let your attention move freely to whatever experience is strong enough to call it away from the breath—whether it's a thought, a sound, a sensation, an image, or a mental state. See if you can stay connected to this experience with affectionate awareness, noting with curiosity and interest what happens to it upon observation.

When the other experience is no longer predominant, return your attention to the breath.

You might also note and label more subtle background mental states, such as calm, boredom, doubt, or apprehension, without needing to change them in any way.

In the last few minutes of this meditation, take a moment to reflect on what matters most to you. Without overthinking, editing, or slipping into rumination, see what simple value or quality bubbles up to the surface of your mind. It might be kindness, or generosity, or authenticity. And now set an intention, like charting a course for a boat, to invite more moments of this quality into your life for the remainder of the day.

Practice Log

For each day that you do the practice of awareness of breath, thoughts, and mental states, fill in the following log. Keeping track of your insights with the practices will help you integrate what you learn from your experiences over time. (Additional copies of this log can be found at http://www.newharbinger.com/28 395—see the very back of this book for download instructions.) download instructions.)

Date and time	What stood out with this practice?

Meditation in Motion: Walking with Anger

Because anger may be hard to sit with, sometimes walking mindfully with anger can be easier. Find a place where you have room to simply walk back and forth, maybe twenty paces or so. Feel free to go outside.

Start walking mindfully, feeling your feet connecting with the ground and your breath gently coming in and out of your body as you walk. Maintaining a steady pace, bring to mind a difficult situation that triggers anger in you, and see if you can allow yourself to really move in close and just feel the anger while keeping a steady rhythm of walking and breathing. For many people, evoking the intention of holding the anger tenderly, as a mother holds her newborn child, allows them to move in close and feel the discomfort of the anger. Whenever you need to take a break, simply walk and bring your attention fully to the breath, and then return to the practice. Be very gentle with yourself in this exercise, and always remember to work progressively, starting with less intense emotions first.

You might even hold your hand at your heart. The intention is to actually feel the anger, not to simply observe it from a distance. See if the anger, when held in awareness in this way, gives way to another feeling, and perhaps yet another, and just meet those feelings with as much sensitivity and kindness as you can. Allow the feelings to arise and pass, and notice the tendency of the mind to want to solidify the feelings with stories and justifications. Many people find it helpful to use a quiet label in the mind for whatever feeling they are noticing. If other things call your attention away as you walk, just notice them and escort your attention back to your feelings.

Finally, leave a few minutes to simply walk and breathe mindfully, feeling your body becoming totally renewed by each in-breath and releasing any tension from this exercise through each out-breath.

Field Observation: Anger Diary

During this week, notice what triggers anger in your day-to-day life. When anger arises, notice how it feels in the body, and see what happens when you intervene with a few deep breaths or mindfulness of anger. Use the spaces below to write down your observations.

Date and time	Trigger	Body sensations	What happens when you apply breath awareness or mindfulness of anger?

After you have recorded at least a few situations in which you felt anger, look for patterns in your anger triggers. This can be useful and even revelatory information, because anger often seems to be the fault of someone else. Seeing our own patterns can prepare us both to better regulate emotions and to take more responsibility for our own reactivity. Common anger triggers include disrespect, embarrassment, rudeness, entitlement, and selfishness. Whatever your triggers are, see if you can bring kindness to the source of those triggers as well as to the suffering of anger itself.

Although anger is an emotion that's hard to deal with, there's something beautiful and humbling in the recognition that it's just a part of human nature. In one way or another, human beings everywhere have to deal with their difficult emotions and try to learn to relate to them in a way that makes peace and happiness possible.

We'd like to close this chapter with a Cherokee story. A boy tells his grandfather about his anger at a friend who had done him an injustice. His grandfather replies: "I too, at times, have felt great hate for those who have taken so much, with no sorrow for what they do. But hate wears you down, and does not hurt your enemy. It's like taking poison and wishing your enemy would die. I have struggled with these feelings many times. My son, the battle is between two wolves inside us all. One wolf brings happiness. It is joy, peace, love, hope, serenity, humility, kindness, benevolence, empathy, generosity, truth, compassion, and faith. But the other wolf ... ah! The littlest thing will send him into a fit of temper. He fights everyone, all the time, for no reason. He cannot think because his anger and hate are so great. Sometimes it is hard to live with these two wolves inside me, for both of them try to dominate my spirit."

The boy looked intently into his grandfather's eyes and asked, "Which one wins, Grandfather?"

The grandfather smiled and quietly said, *"The one I feed."*

Be gentle with yourself as you continue and deepen your practice. Training in mindfulness is remembering that every moment is an opportunity to practice peace, no matter the circumstances. Our thoughts, words, and actions are food for the wolves we all have inside. There's no need for guilt when you notice you're feeding the angry wolf (we all do this, and guilt won't help). Instead, give yourself the freedom to learn from your experience and keep practicing. Trust that it's the small—often invisible—steps that take you forward.

Chapter 9

Cultivating Kindness

TAPPING INTO THE OCEAN OF LOVE WITHIN

Kindness is a basic quality of the heart that involves connection, appreciation, and wishing happiness for oneself and others. Kindness implies not only rejoicing in the happiness of beings (including oneself), but helping to create the conditions for happiness to arise. When kindness is present in the conversation we hold with ourselves and others, emotional balance becomes more easily accessible and sustainable.

In the last chapter, we focused on learning ways to relate to anger mindfully. Without having to suppress or deny anger, it's possible to nourish healing emotions such as love, compassion, joy, and happiness. Because it's impossible to experience kindness and anger in the exact same moment, kindness can be seen as a direct antidote to anger—and the more we cultivate kindness, the more available it becomes. This strategy doesn't work, however, if kindness is being used as a way to suppress anger. When that kind of instrumentality creeps in, the anger simply goes underground, and is likely to pop up later in the form of resentment, or physical symptoms. The cultivation of kindness that we're talking about can be better framed as *remembering* something that we already know. Most contemplative traditions and psychologists agree that kindness is part of human nature, and many would argue that we share this basic instinct for care and connection with all mammals.

Practicing kindness and compassion involves tapping into the ocean of love that is already available within the heart, rather than adding something extra. It's about unleashing rather than fabricating. When we connect with kindness, it's possible to have greater agency over our own happiness, to improve our relationships, and to find the freedom to respond rather than react. Uncovering and cultivating these basic qualities of the heart also makes it easier to meditate and increases one's ability to empathize with others. All of these benefits support emotional balance.

Awakening Kindness

The human mind and body are designed to thrive in kindness. Love, care, and kindness activate the soothing-calming system of our brains, which makes us feel safe, content, and playful. This system is primed in us from a very early age—while we're still in the womb—and it's activated throughout our life cycle whenever we spend time with people with whom we feel emotionally connected, attuned, and safe. When we receive and offer kindness to ourselves and others, the pituitary gland releases oxytocin, the neurohormone of bonding and connection, which elicits feelings of trust, affiliation, and connection, and reduces sensitivity to threats in the fear-and-stress circuitry of the brain. This is why kindness is crucial not only in maintaining sound psychological health, but also in recovering from difficult experiences.

The healing power of kindness is reflected in the fact that one of the strongest predictors of success in psychotherapy is the capacity of the therapist to hold her clients in what psychologist Carl Rogers (1957) calls "unconditional positive regard"—a relational quality characterized by deep empathy and unconditional acceptance of others. As you might have already noticed from your own meditation practice, it's also possible to offer this kind of presence to ourselves; and doing so also activates the soothing-calming system.

When we sit in meditation we practice befriending ourselves, offering an unconditional, nonjudgmental positive regard to all that arises. The kindness and compassion meditations we'll explore, which are traditionally introduced once the mind has gained some grounding and stability through mindfulness, are supercharged formulas to strengthen these natural capacities of the mind and heart.

In general, kindness arises from noticing lovable qualities in ourselves and in others. But, as we'll explore soon, this capacity to see what is good and lovable in ourselves and others, and to see the highest potential that resides within each of us, is not fixed. To the contrary, it's a highly trainable quality. In this chapter, we'll introduce different ways to tap into the stream of kindness, and from there we'll explore ways to expand this natural capacity. For now, let's begin with an experiment that will help us dive into direct experience.

Experiment: Recognizing Natural Kindness

Choose a comfortable seated position. Take three deep breaths, gently relaxing your body and connecting with the natural spaciousness of the mind.

Bring to your mind the image of someone who naturally makes you smile. It could be a person—like a dear child, a good friend, or a kind teacher or mentor—but it could also be a pet. Any being who naturally inspires a sense of appreciation, joy, love, or gratitude will do. Evoke this being's presence in front of you with as much detail as you can, or remember a specific situation in which you felt really connected with this being.

If you work with a specific memory, remember what was happening and how you were feeling. Take a couple of minutes to feel whatever arises in your experience.

Still holding this image or memory in your mind, notice how your body responds. How does it feel in your body? Recognize the sensations associated with kindness and friendliness in your body. Take a couple of minutes for this and see if you can exaggerate that feeling throughout the entire body.

Finally, bring your attention back to the simplicity of your breath for a minute or two, gently letting go of the images and memories.

Take a moment to reflect on the following questions:

• What stood out to you about this experience?

• Did you experience any changes in your bodily sensations?

• Describe any change that you noticed in any part of your body.

• Was there anything you liked about how it felt?

• Was there anything you disliked about how it felt?

As you might have noticed from the exercises in this book (including this one), a feeling state isn't a simple automatic reaction; it's something that can actually be evoked in different ways, including imagery, memory, intention setting, and inner dialogue. A feeling state characterized by friendliness, goodwill, and kindness creates noticeable changes in the body that can affect both your immediate sense of well-being and your long-term health. When states such as anger, resentment, or fear become chronic, they also have the power to negatively impact our health—for example, increasing the risk of illness by weakening the cardiovascular and immune systems.

No matter which emotion we're working with, the mind tends to focus on the external object, situation, or person as the apparent cause of the emotion. But the truth is that the main cause of how we feel about *anything* resides in our mental and emotional habits. Furthermore, the immediate recipient of the emotion is the person feeling it. If the real source of emotions were other people, everyone would feel the same way about a particular person, but experience tells us otherwise: our best friends can be other people's enemies, and even someone we'd consider rude and offensive may well be someone else's best friend. Ultimately, we're responsible for—and the receivers of—the emotions and attitudes we develop. This is why, to paraphrase the Dalai Lama, practicing kindness toward others is *wisely selfish*—we are the main recipients of any kindness we offer to others.

Close and Far Enemies of Kindness

Although kindness has an easily recognizable *far enemy* (hatred), it also has a *close enemy,* an imposter that can masquerade as kindness, but really isn't. This is *self-centered attachment.* Certain kinds of attachment are truly helpful (such as the parent-child bond), but there is another type of attachment that often gets confused with kindness. This is sometimes called conditional love or self-centered love, and it occurs when we're kind to others while at the same time wanting something in return, or when we're expecting a particular outcome from someone in exchange for our love. This kind of interaction has an "if" at its core: "I will love you if..."; "I will accept you if..."

Another way to make the distinction between love and attachment has to do with how much focus is on the self, rather than on the other person. Sometimes, though the words or actions seem to be about the welfare of the other, the focus is really on the self—the needs and desires of the person expressing love. ("I love you, therefore I need you to...") It's not uncommon to engage in this kind of exchange with *ourselves* as well as with others, conditioning our self-acceptance on meeting standards of who we *should* be, how we *should* act, or how we *should* look.

With awareness, we can begin to untangle this complexity, examine our motives, and choose the most wholesome motive to drive our actions. In this way, we can let go of any attachment to outcome. If suffering is the gap between our expectations and reality, becoming aware of our expectations and then dropping them is an important practice for reducing suffering in ourselves and others.

In contrast to self-centered attachment, real kindness involves an unconditional acceptance of others as they are in their own right, without any imposition of our own, self-centered vision of who they should be.

Granted, this is easier said than done—particularly with our partners and children—and this is why we can't overemphasize the idea of *practice, training,* or *cultivation,* instead of approaching the matter in terms of moral dictates ("Thou shalt be kind"). Perhaps the easiest way to destroy any inclination to be genuinely kind is to demand it of ourselves or others.

Exercise: Gratitude Diary

One important strategy for cultivating kindness in our lives involves connecting with a sense of gratitude and appreciation. Noticing what is working, what is good in ourselves and others, and what is beautiful in our surroundings and in people around us helps us to "take in the good" and to savor the gifts that are already here. The idea of the gratitude diary is to access a mind-set of abundance and appreciation and to diminish the mind's tendency to focus on what's lacking. In psychology, gratitude has been associated with not only increased happiness, life satisfaction, and well-being, and decreased depression, stress, and anxiety (Emmons and McCullough 2003; Hanson and Mendius 2009; Hanson 2013), but also relational well-being, empathy, and altruistic behavior (Bartlett and DeSteno 2006).

Here's the invitation: Each night for the next seven days, write down five things, people, or events that you feel grateful for. These could be things that went well in your day, beauty that you encountered, positive qualities that you noticed in yourself or others, and so on. Keep this book or a diary and pen right next to your bed so that you can fill up your daily entry before falling asleep. If you forget to do it one night, you can catch up first thing the following morning.

As you do this exercise through the week, notice how the intention to purposefully find things to be grateful for affects your mind, your mood, and your perceptions.

186

Day 1	1.
	2.
	3.
	4.
	5.

Day 2	1.
	2.
	3.
	4.
	5.

Day 3	1.
	2.
	3.
	4.
	5.

Day 4	1.
	2.
	3.
	4.
	5.

Day 5	1.
	2.
	3.
	4.
	5.

Day 6	1.
	2.
	3.
	4.
	5.

Day 7	1.
	2.
	3.
	4.
	5.

When you've finished this exercise (after seven days), read the full list of things you were grateful for, and take a moment to savor them and take them in. What do you notice? What did you discover from this exercise?

Finally, if you feel inspired to do so, feel free to extend this practice to longer periods (perhaps twenty-one days, or a full month), using the downloadable version of the gratitude diary that's available at http://www.newharbinger.com/28395. You can even turn it into a lifelong habit! lifelong habit!

Shifting Mind-sets: From Scarcity to Abundance

The Pali term that is commonly translated into English as "kindness," "loving-kindness," "unconditional love," or simply "friendliness," is the word *metta.* In the earliest Buddhist scriptures on emotion regulation, it is told that a Brahmin—a devotee of Brahma, the Hindu god—came to the Buddha and asked him how he could merge his mind with the mind of Brahma. In a beautiful gesture of empathy, the Buddha didn't respond with something like "Sorry, we don't believe in gods here, this is a nontheistic tradition." Instead, he approached the question in the same language as the Brahmin, practicing the Rogerian "unconditional positive regard" with Brahma's devotee 2500 years before Rogers.

The Buddha told him that to merge his mind with Brahma's and to really abide with him, he had to practice the "Brahmaviharas," or "Brahma abodes." These are: *metta* (unconditional friendliness), *karuna* (empathy and compassion), *mudita* (altruistic joy), and *upekkha* (equanimity). The Buddha advised the Brahmin to cultivate these four qualities in his mind and heart, because a mind endowed with these qualities couldn't be too far from Brahma.

These four qualities of the mind are also sometimes called the *four immeasurables*—a term that conveys the idea that their cultivation isn't a zero-sum game in which abundance for some means scarcity for others. Many people erroneously think of kindness and compassion as finite resources that we can run out of after a time, like food in the cupboard. In this case, there's often both a sense of competition for limited resources and a "tit for tat" expectation. If resources are limited, it's only natural that anxieties and expectations arise; these anxieties and expectations disappear when the kindness and compassion resources are viewed as unlimited. Contemplative traditions assert that the more we cultivate these qualities in ourselves, the more abundant and accessible they become for us *and* for others. In fact, as we know from recent research on positive emotions (Fredrickson 2014, for example), these qualities are quite contagious. You are probably already quite aware of this from your own experiences.

If we look a little closer, equanimity could be seen as a spacious ground offering balance and stability, a basis of operation from which a person remains engaged and responsive, but is freed from the reactivity of attachment. This equanimity is greatly enhanced by training in nonjudgmental awareness of moment-to-moment experience, as you've been doing in the mindfulness practices. Without this stable basis, love would easily turn into self-serving attachment, compassion into pity, and joy into mania or addiction—we would get the close enemies instead of the real thing.

The other three qualities or "abodes" (love, compassion, and joy) could also be seen as variations of the same thing—different packages for the same basic warm, caring quality of the heart. Love is this basic energy expressed as goodwill and the wish for beings to be happy; altruistic joy is how this energy responds to the happiness, success, and beauty of others; and compassion is the natural response of this basic caring energy when it encounters suffering.

Finally, true equanimity is also sustained by the energy of a caring heart, because when this loving energy is absent, equanimity turns into its own close enemy—distant indifference. Summing it all up, the Buddha's recipe for emotional balance seems to include a good deal of equanimity, to keep attachment and aversion at bay, and a heart that is warm, open, tender, and caring. Simple, but not easy, and this is exactly why we need practice.

Let's focus now on the kindness meditation practice. Before starting, remember that, like forgiveness, true feelings of kindness can't be forced. They can only be invited through the setting of intention and the steadiness of a consistent practice. Although the focus of this practice is to nourish kindness, appreciation, and gratitude, other feelings will also arise, and this is both normal and important.

If sadness arises, it can be embraced as part of a grief process, and as a natural aspect of how the heart heals itself. If anger arises, see if you can hold it with tenderness, not forcing anything, while giving yourself permission to return to the object of meditation or to a category that feels more comfortable for you, such as a child or a pet. If the heart feels "dry," know that even by reflecting on kindness, something is happening within you, much as with the intention-setting practice. Remember that whatever we attend to is our reality. When we're focusing on kindness, even if the emotion isn't present, we're watering the seeds of kindness within.

Practice Plan, Week 6

Meditation Practice: Kindness

(*recording available at* http://www.newharbinger.com /28395)

Some of the language for both this practice and the compassion practice in chapter 11 comes from our esteemed colleague, Kelly McGonigal.

Find a place where you can be quiet and undisturbed, and position the body in a way that feels comfortable while also allowing you to remain alert. (It's quite difficult to generate feelings of kindness when the body is in pain.) When practiced consistently, this guided meditation can be the source of great joy and generosity. Again, a script is offered in addition to the audio recording for those who either prefer to read and then practice on their own, or for those who like to reinforce their understanding by reading before listening to the guided meditation.

• Begin by bringing your attention to the area around your physical heart—noticing how this area gently expands or fills when you breathe in, and how it relaxes when you breathe out. For a few breaths, imagine that you could inhale directly into the center of your chest, expanding the chest, lungs, and heart. Imagine that you could exhale directly from the center of your chest.

• Gather your attention on the sensations of the breath in the chest, bringing extra gentleness to any tender feelings you might become aware of. As best you can, take the next few minutes to direct your attention to the sensations around the heart as you breathe. Whenever you notice the mind has wandered to thoughts, images, sounds, or sensations in *other* parts of the body, gently escort it back to the sensation in the chest as it rises with the in-breath and falls with the out-breath.

- Now, imagine yourself as a very young child or at an age that you can remember from your childhood. Like all children, you were innocent, and hungry for love—wanting to do your best, and not always understanding what happened when you fell short of others' expectations. Imagine seeing this child version of yourself in front of you. What might you wish for this child? Do you naturally want this child to be happy, to be safe, to be loved and fulfilled? Allow any feelings of tenderness and appreciation toward the "childhood you" to permeate your heart, and then silently repeat these phrases for yourself as a child:

  "May you be happy ... May you be loved ... May you know peace and joy..."

- Now, bring to mind something that you appreciate about yourself. It could be something you did, or a personal quality. If this is hard for you, imagine what a parent or a good friend might say about you. Take a moment to acknowledge this aspect of yourself. Offer yourself the warmth and generosity of your own friendship as you silently repeat these phrases, feeling free to alter the language if it helps you to connect with the feeling behind the words:

  "May I be happy ... May I give and receive all the love that I need ... May I know peace and joy."

- Pause and gently breathe in and out.

- Now, bring to mind someone you care about, such as a family member or a friend, someone who naturally brings a smile to your face. Try to vividly feel his (let's assume a male person) presence in front of you. Imagine seeing him through the eyes of your heart. Notice how you feel when you think about him. In close relationships, there's often a history of conflict and complexity. For now, as best you can, just notice any feelings of gratitude, affection, or warmth that you feel for this loved one. When you see him through the eyes of your heart, what do you wish for him? Silently repeat the following phrases in order to guide yourself into the source of goodwill in your own heart:

  "May you be happy ... May you give and receive all the love that you need ... May you know peace and joy."

- Pause and gently breathe in and out.

- Now, bring to mind someone you recognize but have no special sense of either closeness or conflict with. It could be a checker at the grocery store or a barista at the coffee shop; or maybe someone you work with but don't know well. Notice how you feel when you think about this person. Consider the fact that, just like you, this person has had ups and downs in her life (here, let's assume this person is a woman). And imagine that, just like you, she is an object of deep concern to someone; she is a child to someone; a parent, a spouse, or a dear friend to someone. Just like you, she has goals and dreams. Just like you, she wants to love and be loved; to contribute and to be appreciated. Now, hold a sense of this stranger as a whole human being, with a life every bit as textured and nuanced as your own, seeing her through the eyes of the heart and silently repeating:

"May you be happy ... May you give and receive all the love that you need ... May you know peace and joy."

- Pause and gently breathe in and out.

- Now, bring to mind a person you have some difficulty or discomfort with. Maybe it's someone with whom you don't get along or someone you feel in competition with. Maybe it's someone you think has caused you harm. It's not necessary to choose the *most* difficult person in your life. In fact, it can be more effective to begin with minor irritations and slowly work your way up to the really challenging people. Notice how you feel when you think about this person. Try seeing this challenging person through the eyes of the heart. Consider the possibility that all unskillful actions can be understood as tragic expressions of unmet needs. Just like you, this person has goals and dreams. Just like you, this person is an object of deep concern to someone; he or she is a child to someone; a parent, a spouse, or a dear friend to someone. Just like you, this person wants to love and be loved; to contribute and to be appreciated.

- Remember that it's possible to wish people well without forgiving their actions or reconciling with them. Bearing all this in mind, silently repeat these phrases, focusing on the human being rather than the story of what that person did to you: "May you be happy ... May you give and receive all the love that you need ... May you know peace and joy."

- Now, contemplate this thought: "My life is supported in many ways, big and small, by countless other people—including those I consider to be friends or strangers—and even by those with whom I experience conflict. For all of us, in ways we will never truly know, our lives are supported by countless others." Now consider that in ways you may never know, you, too, play a similar supportive role in the lives of countless others. Let your mind abide in this awareness of deep appreciation and interconnectedness for a moment.

- Now, continue to expand the scope of your awareness to all those around you—imagining that your heart is like an energy field that can expand in all directions, wider and wider, to include everyone who lives in your state, on your continent, and on this planet. Letting feelings of care and kindness extend to those who are suffering and to those who are happy, to those who are old, and perhaps dying in this very moment, and to those just being born, with their whole lives ahead of them. To those with great wealth, and to those barely scraping by—appreciating this great mysterious web of life that connects us all, and the fundamental aspirations we share with all beings. Silently extending the following phrases as an offering to all beings: "May all beings be happy ... May all beings give and receive all the love that they need ... May all beings know peace and joy."

- Rest for a few moments in this state of open-hearted, open-minded kindness. Welcome any sense of peace and happiness that this practice might bring to your body and mind.

- Conclude this meditation by dedicating your positive effort to the peace and wellbeing of all beings throughout the world, including yourself. Know that just as you are practicing to deepen and broaden your capacity for kindness, countless others are extending their own kindness and goodwill toward you.

Practice Log

For each day that you do the kindness meditation practice, fill in the following log (which you can also download from http://www.newharbinger.com/28395). Keeping track of your insights with the practices will help you integrate what you learn from your experiences overtime. insights with the practices will help you integrate what you learn from your experiences over time.

Date and time	What stood out with this practice?

Field Observation: Kindness

Kindness "on the go": Experiment with sending kindness to others you come in contact with throughout the day, noticing how you feel as you do this. If you wish, you can use the same phrases as in the kindness meditation practice, repeating one or more of them silently in your mind: "May you be happy ... May you know peace and joy."

Notice what happens in yourself and in your environment when you do this.

Field Notes

Exercising the "good eye": Look for beauty and goodness in unexpected places or in people you would normally dismiss as ugly or uninteresting. Look for things or events that could be a source of appreciation in your day-to-day life. The key element here is to see others in the same way you would like to be seen by them.

Field Notes

Kindness is a quality of the heart that brings happiness when received from others, but through intentional cultivation, we begin to realize that it brings even more happiness and well-being when we offer it. Each time we offer kindness we're sending ourselves the message that we already have this quality within us, with plenty to spare.

Besides the formal kindness meditation and the field observations of this week, see if you can invite the attitude of kindness as the basic tone for the way you relate to your life as a whole. In any given situation, when things go right or wrong, when you get what you want or when you don't, simply ask yourself: What would it mean to invite kindness into this situation?

Finally, remember that we all wish to be seen with the eyes of kindness. Here is the advice of the fourteenth-century Persian poet and mystic Hafiz:

> Admit something: Everyone you see, you say to them, "Love me."
> Of course you do not do this out loud, otherwise someone would call the cops.
> Still though, think about this, this great pull in us to connect.
> Why not become the one who lives with a full moon in each eye that is always saying, with that sweet moon language,
> What every other eye in this world is dying to hear?
>
> (Ladinsky 2010, 282)

Chapter 10

Working with Fear

THE ART OF FACING THE MONSTER

Fear is one of the main challenges that we encounter on the path of cultivating emotional balance. When we're afraid, our outlook, imagination, and personal resources shrink, and we begin to inhabit the world from a diminished sense of self—when we're afraid, we become smaller than we are. Most of us can probably relate to the experience of having to face something daunting the following week—perhaps a medical procedure, or meeting a difficult person or a deadline. The mere anticipation of this event can cast a gloomy shade of preoccupation over the entire week, taking away the joy of positive experiences that go unnoticed under the weight of anticipatory fear.

On the other hand, fear can be an unexpectedly invaluable ally on our path to personal growth and emotional balance, precisely because the experience of fear points directly to the tendency to resist and control rather than to accept experience as it is. Fear and its intense bodily and mental correlates are like inner exclamation marks telling us that there's potential for growth and integration right here, in the midst of our fears. This suggests something that might seem counterintuitive: that to work with our fears we need to learn to get closer to them, instead of running away, which is what the mind and the body are trained to do. The invitation in this chapter is to explore the possibility of cultivating a radically different relationship to what frightens you.

In mythical stories, there's usually a point at which the hero or heroine has to face something really frightening—a dragon or monster—before reaching a deeper level of personal integration, often symbolized as encountering the confined beloved or finding a treasure, a key, or a precious ring. When we train ourselves to face our monsters, we gradually become capable of holding our fears and exploring them within the spaciousness of mindfulness. As we begin to explore our fears in this way and learn to identify them for what they are, new levels of freedom become available. This newly gained freedom is born not out of getting rid of fear, but from the certainty that there's a vaster space in which fear can arise and pass away, like any other experience. But let's take things one step at a time and explore what fear actually is.

What Is Fear? Why Do We Experience It?

Fear is an emotion, and as such, it's a perfectly normal human experience. Fear can be provoked by universal or personal triggers, and both kinds of triggers have to do with the threat of harm, either physical or psychological. Universal triggers involve things such as an object hurtling quickly through space, appearing as if it might hit us if we don't duck; the sudden loss of physical support, making us feel as if we might fall; and the threat of physical pain (Ekman 2003).

As humans, we can learn to become frightened of nearly anything, so personal triggers vary widely. After watching an Alfred Hitchcock movie, we might feel fear when a door is opened, because the sound of the door is associated with something scary that happened in the movie. A friend of Gonzalo's who's in her early eighties simply can't step into a room if there's a cat in it, and even the mere mention of the word "cat" makes her face go pale—not because she ever had a traumatic encounter with a feline, but because someone told her a horror story that involved a demonic cat when she was only five! We can become afraid of nearly anything, and just knowing this can foster compassion for others' seemingly irrational fears (and our own).

Even if it were possible to be without fear, it wouldn't really be desirable, because you wouldn't be able to evaluate danger and respond in appropriate ways. Fear is nature's gift to secure survival. The brain and the body evolved with a sophisticated mechanism to experience fear and react to it. Thanks to this innate capacity, we have been able to deal with predators, adverse climate, and other environmental pressures throughout our evolutionary history. From this perspective, fear is simply the way the body and mind evolved to recognize threats and prepare to deal with them effectively. But although the capacity to experience fear is adaptive, there seems to be a mismatch between the life-threatening challenges of our ancestors and the kinds of fear triggers that modern humans typically have to face.

Experiment: Breathing and Observing Fear

Whenever you become aware that fear, anxiety, or worry has spontaneously arisen (it's probably not happening right now), bring to mind this experiment:

Simply take three deep breaths and note what happens in the mind and the body. Notice what happens to the fear-anxious-worry reaction. Does it stay the same? Does it change? If so, how? Then, when you can, write your responses below.

Consider for a moment the things and events that produce stress, anxiety, or fear in your day-to-day life. It's likely that if you managed to set some time aside to read this book, your fears aren't going to be triggered by dangerous predators lurking in the back yard or leaping from the screen of your Kindle or iPad. Modern fears are more often related to things like dealing with a difficult person at work, meeting a deadline, or situations that evoke social anxiety, such as the fear of rejection or shame. Although it's unlikely that a deadline or having to respond to fifty emails in a single day will prove fatal, the body still responds to these perceived stressors through a chain reaction that prepares us to *fight, to flee, or to freeze.*

To make things a bit more complex, we don't just feel fear in response to external events. Internal experiences such as thoughts or emotions can also trigger the fear reaction; a thought about something can be—and often is—scarier than the thing itself. Human brains are equipped with a sophisticated time-traveling and virtual-reality machine: the neocortex. This is a blessing and a curse because it allows us to plan the future or imagine different scenarios, but it also endows us with the capacity to spend a goodly amount of time and energy rehashing or rehearsing rather than dealing with what's actually present. If you've ever suffered from insomnia, you'll recognize that even on a quiet night in a dark cozy room, it just takes having a mind to worry about the most incredible things—things that may seem insignificant in the light of day. As Thomas Jefferson once wrote in a letter to John Adams: "How much pain have cost us the evils which have never happened!" (Shapiro 2006, 395).

Cognitive distortions such as "black-and-white thinking" tend to accompany the emotion of fear. These served a productive purpose with the kinds of fears our ancestors faced: When confronted with a tiger, it's not so useful to search the brain's hard drive for what

Wikipedia might say, or the *Animal Planet* episode you just watched; rather, survival would demand that thinking be reduced to "tiger-bad-run!" Today, however, black-and-white thinking can impair one's ability to respond effectively to interpersonal threat, and this is what most commonly triggers the fear response. If we're afraid of a meeting with a colleague or supervisor, for example, it's essential to bear in mind all the complexity and subtlety of both past and present circumstances. It's hard to negotiate anything effectively without seeing the other person's point of view, whereas experiencing empathy for the tiger would likely result in your speedy demise.

Fear and the Body

Whether the stressor is internal or external, really life-threatening or just a boogeyman, the body responds with a whole cascade of reactions. These reactions are hardwired and were designed to move us to safety in the event of danger or threat, which is why they are often collectively referred to as the *fight-or-flight* response. Though the phrase *fight or flight* is commonly used, another hardwired reaction is to *freeze* in the face of perceived danger, as many animals do when startled. Our response depends on what past experiences have taught us about how to protect ourselves in similar situations.

If one is unable to freeze, hide, or flee, it's common to become angry at whatever appears threatening. In these situations, mindfulness can be very helpful, since awareness can be directed to the anger when it arises. It's also possible to become afraid of our own anger, or angry at ourselves for becoming afraid—it's helpful to bring mindful awareness to these occurrences as well (more on this in the following chapter). Whether we fight, flee, or freeze, a chain of both internal and external reactions takes hold automatically and often unconsciously. This prepares the body for action against the perceived threat and can be life-saving in truly threatening situations, helping the mind and body to become physiologically ready to deal with the threat.

The amygdala, a tiny but powerful alarm center in our midbrain whose role it is to detect risk signals in the environment, sends chemical and electrical messages to produce a state of hyperarousal, activating the hypothalamus, pituitary, and adrenal glands. In this state, we might experience rapid heartbeat, muscle tension, heightened emotions, elevated blood pressure, sweating, and increased alertness. This response is quite appropriate and healthy when it's occasional and it helps us to deal with specific challenges. However, this automatic reaction mode is also activated by triggers that don't pose a threat to physical survival, such as speaking in public or taking an exam. The fear response can also be triggered by perceived threats to our status, belief system, or sense of control.

When this state of hyperarousal, characterized by psychological and physiological tension, anxiety, insomnia, and fatigue, occurs repeatedly over time, we might be cultivating an anxious mood, which is longer lived than the fear reaction, lasting hours or days. If we're in an anxious mood, the emotion of fear in response to a trigger is more likely to arise. We might not know the reason for the anxious mood, but we can generally point to something specific that triggers the fear.

Paul Ekman (2003) names seven primary and universal emotions: fear, anger, surprise, sadness, contempt, disgust, and happiness. Each of these emotions represents a "family" of emotions that have the same flavor but vary in intensity or tone. Other emotions in the fear family include worry, terror, nervousness, uneasiness, anxiety, and apprehensiveness.

When anxiety becomes part of our normal landscape of experience, we might not even be aware that our life is being lived—chronically—from a mind and body dominated by fear. But the body will still register the consequences of this state and present symptoms such as high blood pressure, sleep disorders, and chronic headaches or backaches.

Sometimes there's nothing we can do when confronted with the threat of harm. If there's nothing to do but wait to see if we survive, fear can escalate into terror. At other times, when something can be done about a threat, focusing on the task at hand can reduce the feeling of fear. For example, if the car we're driving begins to swerve off the road, we can (and probably will) adjust the steering wheel to compensate. As we steer, fear may lessen—we're concentrating on what needs to be done. However, if we realize we can't control the car, the fear may quickly escalate into panic (Ekman 2003).

While responding to an immediate threat often reduces physical pain sensations, worrying about an impending threat tends to magnify pain and often leads to increased vigilance and muscular tension. These effects can be cumulative and can lead to a variety of physical problems.

As with other emotions, there's a refractory period associated with fear. When fear arises, it's hard, if not impossible, to feel or think about anything else, and, interestingly, our cognition is "gated" in such a way that we see only that which confirms our fear. For example, when watching a scary movie we may become hyperalert to sounds and even misinterpret the sound of the wind or the creak of the house as a threat or an omen. If fear becomes a constant in our lives, we might actually be losing perspective on important chunks of reality that don't fit our fears.

Now let's go back to direct experience through an exercise. Some ways of working with fear involve waiting until fear shows up. Here we'll introduce a different, more proactive approach in which we actually invite fear in, taking the unpredictability out of the experience and allowing us to be more in control.

Exercise: Relived Fear

This exercise offers a guided visualization in which you'll remember a time when you were afraid in order to find the "inner geography"—the physical coordinates—of fear in the body. Understanding what fear feels like in the body, and becoming comfortable with those sensations, can help in recognizing and labeling fear in the moment it arises, allowing for the space to respond rather than react. Remember that there's never a right or wrong way to experience a visualization. Also, you are in charge of how strongly you evoke the emotion, and even if a very strong feeling arises, it will quickly pass. We suggest you read the complete instructions below to familiarize yourself with them. Then you can come back and read each point and take a minute or two to practice it before moving to the next.

• Sit in meditation posture, in a relaxed yet alert position, with your hands resting comfortably and your eyes gently closed. Check in with the body, feeling the places where it makes contact with the chair or the floor.

• Take three deep breaths, completely filling the torso with air. Then completely release the breath.

• Now, remember a time when you were scared. Envision and experience what happened, filling in the scene in your mind only enough to exaggerate the feelings in the body. If you notice other feelings, such as anger or disgust, see if you can focus back on the feeling of fear.

• What types of sensations do you feel? Tightness, heat, cold, pressure, tension? Where in your body are you feeling them? Stay with the feelings as best you can, adding details to the scene if you need to in order to experience the feeling of fear. You may be tempted to try to push it away. Instead, put out the welcome mat for it, investigating how it feels in the body and observing the thoughts it evokes, without getting carried away by those thoughts.

• If you can, open up to this feeling with compassion, cradling it with kindness and tenderness. How would you respond to a child who was terrified? As adults, we continue to have this feeling, but often condemn it and judge ourselves as weak for having it. What is it that you truly need when you feel afraid? Can you offer that to yourself?

• Take three deep, full breaths and slowly bring your attention back to your surroundings. And as you are ready, open your eyes.

When you're done with the exercise, jot down some notes in the table below: Where did you experience fear in the body? Which sensations did you notice? Which thoughts appeared in your mind? Which emotions emerged?

Bodily sensations	Thoughts	Emotions

The relived fear exercise introduces some of the elements of a mindful approach to fear, such as feeling the sensations in the body, and observing the thoughts and emotions related to fear from a nonreactive attitude and cultivating the courage of opening instead of closing our awareness and our hearts to what's difficult. Let's explore in more detail what it means to embrace fear, anxiety, and worry with mindful awareness.

Holding Our Fears with Mindful Awareness

As we discussed above, fear is part of our emotional repertoire—it's just a biologically determined reaction to threat that we share not only with all other humans, but also with all other animals. This suggests that when you feel afraid you can remind yourself that it's neither your fault nor a personal plot against you and you alone; it's just the way the brain and body have evolved over millennia. Of course, this doesn't mean that we can't do anything about our fears. We actually have the freedom to do quite a lot, and most of what can be done involves *how we relate* to the simple experience of fear.

When fear is present, it's common to fixate on the feeling, rather than to perceive it as a transient state that will arise and pass away like any other thought or emotion. Our sense of self tends to contract around fear, and in this way both the fear and the sense of self become more solid than they actually are. The subtle sense of contraction and the desire to control ourselves or our environment when fear is present are what paradoxically get us stuck in fear. This is equally true for anger and sadness, which are also natural movements of emotional energy—it's the contraction and solidification of the feeling that gets us stuck and makes us sick.

With the practice of mindfulness, we gradually learn to soften this contraction around fear. The fast heartbeat and muscular tension might still be there, and scary thoughts might still cross our minds, but we slowly learn to deidentify with fear and begin to identify with the larger field of awareness. Deidentification with fear implies recognizing and remembering something that might seem simple but that's not always easy to remember when we're afraid or worried: "I am not this fear. This fear is not me. I am not this worry. This worry is not me."

Mindful awareness can hold fear just like a mother can hold a frightened child in her lap until the child's fear dissipates. Of course, the mother can't force the child into peace. She can only offer her warmth, holding, acceptance, and patience. Similarly, when we practice mindfulness with our own fears, we learn to mother ourselves, holding our emotions with the same kind of warmth and patience. Sometimes people fear that offering this kind of love to ourselves involves some kind of selfishness or narcissism, but actually the opposite is true. We can only offer our warmth and presence to others if we first learn to offer that kindness to ourselves.

Loving-kindness toward ourselves, understood as the capacity to embrace with nonjudgmental awareness those aspects that we are so tempted to reject or deny, is perhaps the greatest antidote to fear, and loving-kindness is integral to mindfulness. Much fear comes from the often unconscious, unchallenged, and limiting belief that something is fundamentally wrong with us, and that we should be different than we are. When we begin to cultivate lovingkindness with ourselves and soften our self-judgment, the sense of being threatened (even from external circumstances) diminishes considerably.

Incorporating Mindfulness into the Fear Reaction Cycle

Through the practice of paying attention to moment-to-moment experience in a nonjudgmental manner, it's possible to insert mindfulness as a wedge at any point in the fear reaction, creating the necessary space for responding instead of reacting to fear. From the moment fear is triggered—either by an external stressor (such as encountering a difficult person) or an internal stressor (such as fear of being judged by others)—the perception of the trigger *itself* can be altered by observing what is happening inside and outside the body without automatically engaging in the cascade of interpretations, judgments, thoughts, and emotions about what's going on.

This isn't about judging as safe something that we perceive as threatening, and it's not about liking or approving of the trigger. It's more like removing the fuel from a blazing fire by seeing the situation clearly instead of seeing it as something solid, monolithic, and catastrophic. We might see that, by simply turning toward the physical sensations and labeling them, it's possible to avoid getting lost in the story or even making it worse with an unconscious cycle of thoughts, emotions, and physical sensations.

Of course, the perceived intensity of the trigger will affect our ability to bring mindful awareness to what's arising. For a smaller trigger (such as whether we'll be late to a party), it might be possible to become aware early enough to observe how the event is being interpreted and to shift perception so that the fear reaction is obviated. In contrast, when we unconsciously react to an acute and intense trigger (such as an upcoming medical procedure), the experience seems very solid and we rarely notice our distorted interpretations of the trigger—reacting instead as if on autopilot. In these situations, interpretations of the trigger tend to merge with the perception of it. But, with practice, inserting mindfulness wedges becomes not only possible but habitual, even in the face of acute and intense triggers.

By bringing mindful awareness to the perception of what scares you, it's possible to perceive it as something that is less permanent and perhaps less personal than it appears at first glance. When a trigger is seen as fixed and taken personally, the tendency for overidentification and destructive self-talk gets stronger. In this instance, it might be useful to recall seventh-century Indian sage Shantideva's pithy advice in dealing with worries, as recounted in Thondup (1998): "If you can solve your problem, what's the need of worrying? If you can't solve it, what's the use of worrying?"

Although it might be simple to understand what Shantideva says at an intellectual level, the integration of this perspective into real-life situations is not always easy or immediate, not even for people like the monks he was advising. Nevertheless, the practice of applying mindfulness to the perception of fear triggers can be fruitful even from the very first attempts. Although fear and worry will never completely go away, increased awareness helps to both reduce the level of physiological and emotional arousal and to allow a quicker return to balance. The heart might still beat fast and the large muscles might still tense, but gradually a change in the intensity of the reaction can be perceived.

Another important way in which mindfulness can create the space to respond instead of react to the feeling of fear is by allowing access to the full context of the situation, making it possible to find new ways to deal with the perceived threat. As mentioned above, when we are in the grip of an emotion, our field of awareness tends to narrow, limiting perception to *only* those elements in the environment that are relevant to our current emotional state and letting in *only* the information that confirms that emotion. If, instead, we pause and pay attention to what's happening in the present moment both inside and outside the body, we can get a better picture of the whole situation. This makes it possible to take in a variety of cues and to find new options and resources both within and without in order to deal with the threat more effectively.

For example, let's say your car breaks down on the freeway. While in the refractory period, or at the height of the fear response, you might be so scared that you sit frozen in the car, forgetting that you have a cell phone in your purse, flares in your trunk, or a safe shoulder on the side of the road to walk to while the cars whiz by, narrowly missing your car.

Mindfulness isn't only useful in the moment that the experience of fear, worry, or anxiety is occurring. It also helps us become aware of what's going on when we find ourselves turning to distractions or self-destructive behaviors (for example, overeating, overworking, using intoxicating substances, binge-watching television) as a way to avoid discomfort. In these situations, we can become curious about our experience right in that moment, instead of getting stuck in shame, guilt, or self-hatred, which usually serve only to perpetuate the addictive cycle and increase its tenacious hold. Fear is often associated with performance and how we're viewed by others, so flavors of fear, such as anxiety, can arise when we're working on any kind of project that will be seen by our peers. You might, for example, notice a pattern of eating sugar or carbs when working on a project as a way of avoiding anxious feelings.

After learning the mindfulness of mental states practice (next), a student shared an interesting insight. She had noticed for some time that her thoughts were dominated by "planning." But it wasn't until she focused on her emotions that she realized that all these planning thoughts were fueled by anxiety, a form of fear. Planning was a strategy for the mind to try to control the unknowable: the future. And because the future is, in fact, unknowable, a tremendous amount of mental energy can be squandered on this Sisyphean task.

As you can see, there are many ways to apply mindfulness to the experience of fear. Meditation helps establish this mindful response, allowing thinking to slow down and letting us observe what's going on in the mind and body moment by moment. With time, this naturally transfers into the rest of daily life, allowing a new way to handle and relate to fear. We gradually stop being hijacked by the energy of fear, and instead begin to recognize it for what it is ("I know you, my fear"), and if the threat requires an action on our part, this action will arise not from automated habits, but from spaciousness, warmth, and wisdom, making it more effective.

Practice Plan, Week 7

Meditation Practice: Mindfulness of Breath, Thoughts, and Mental States

(*recording available at* http://www.newharbinger.com /28395)

For this practice, go back to the "Mindfulness of Breath, Thoughts, and Mental States" exercise in chapter 8, and try it again in this new context.

Practice Log

For each day that you do the "Mindfulness of Breath, Thoughts, and Mental States" practice, fill in the following log. Download additional copies of the log, if you need them, at http://www.newharbinger.com/28395. Keeping track of your insights with the practices will help you integrate what you learn from your experiences over time. help you integrate what you learn from your experiences over time.

Date and time	What stood out with this practice?

Field Observation: Fear

Fear Triggers

Notice what your fear triggers are. Make a list of the things, events, people, or situations that trigger your fear reaction. You can keep a journal for this, or simply complete the list in the spaces below, adding to it as you become aware of new triggers.

Do you notice any patterns or themes in your fear triggers?

Responding to Fear

Notice moments of fear or uncertainty and see if you can respond, rather than react, to these feelings, perhaps even meeting them with kindness and compassion. Write down some notes from your experiences with this practice.

In this chapter, we've familiarized ourselves with fear—what it is, how and why it gets triggered, and how it affects the mind and the body. Getting closer to and observing fear itself mitigates blame, feelings of inadequacy, or taking fear personally. At the same time, increasing familiarization with our own fears increases our empathy for other people's fears.

Approaching fear with curiosity instead of aversion helps us to work with the fear of fear. Just as the only real way to deal with the monster in the closet is to turn on the lights and see what's actually in there, our fears proliferate in the darkness of unawareness, and can most effectively be dealt with in the light of awareness and with the warmth of kindness.

Of course, it's really hard to develop this kind of awareness when we're already in the grips of fear and our perspective is narrowed by fear's refractory period. This is why it's so important to do the practices on a regular basis. In this way, you'll nurture the seeds of fearlessness and mindfulness within you.

Chapter 11

Awakening Compassion

EMBRACING OUR SHARED VULNERABILITY

Part of the wisdom that's cultivated through contemplative practices involves the experiential recognition of suffering as a normal part of life. No matter how lucky, rich, intelligent, or "good meditator" you are, there will still be plenty of times when you don't get what you want, get what you don't want, are separated from those you love, or have to deal with those you don't like. Also, by its very nature, our human body is subject to sickness, aging, and ultimately death, and so are the bodies of those we love. None of this is personal or anybody's fault; it's simply part of life's ground rules. When life shows its tough side, the mind complains: "Why ME?!" reflecting the ingrained habit of holding on to the illusion of separateness and isolation, which gets really solid when we're hurting. We rarely ask "Why *not* me?" when we don't have a problem.

Because suffering is part of our human experience, it's important to become familiar with it and to practice healthier and more constructive ways to relate to it. In this chapter, we'll explore compassion (and self-compassion) as a response to suffering that is key to sustainable emotional balance. In this context, we won't define compassion as an emotion, a virtue, or an attitude. Instead, we'll simply understand compassion as the natural capacity of the heart to recognize and connect with our own and other's suffering, along with the sincere wish to help relieve it.

The Gift of Vulnerability

Although we might think that recognizing vulnerability and suffering could be disempowering or depressing, the opposite is actually true. We receive an unexpected gift when we stop resisting or denying what's difficult and open ourselves to the truth of suffering. It's the gift of realizing and becoming familiar with the beauty and courage of an open heart, a heart that's able to connect and resonate with life in all its depth, richness, and complexity. The alternative to cultivating an open and compassionate heart isn't to avoid suffering. Instead, it's to spend an insane amount of energy in continually shoring up a self-protective shell that disconnects us from life without actually keeping suffering at bay.

Compassion is the courage to allow our hearts to be cracked open by the crazy beauty and terrible suffering of life, recognizing that it's precisely this openness that allows us to connect authentically with others. Authentic connection only comes from recognizing our shared vulnerability, and all humans are equal in that we share a degree of vulnerability—we all have the capacity to suffer and want to be free from suffering; we all want to be happy and to flourish. In fact, not only do we share this quality with other human beings, but, to a large degree, we share this fragility and desire for happiness with all sentient beings.

At a basic level, compassion invites us to refrain from adding more suffering to an already painful situation. Compassion is about being of help instead of an annoyance to ourselves and others. The Dalai Lama often advises: "If you can't help, at least don't hurt." This might seem obvious, but consider for a moment the ingrained habit many of us have of judging ourselves harshly when things don't go as we expect or when we underperform on a certain task, or of habitually becoming annoyed with others as a reaction to our own distress.

Compassion informed by the nonreactive stability of mindfulness practice has the capacity to stop the cycle of suffering and help transform difficult situations. Even when we can't really fix or do something concrete to alleviate a particular suffering, we always have the freedom to choose how we show up in the world, and when we practice showing up with an open and caring attitude, we can make a real difference even in the most difficult scenarios.

In chapter 9 we explored kindness as the capacity of the heart to rejoice in the happiness of beings. When this same basic caring quality of the heart encounters suffering, it becomes compassion. We could say that compassion is love's response to suffering. While love is the genuine wish to see others safe, happy, and joyful, stemming from a heart that's open, tender, and optimistic, compassion is the genuine wish to see suffering relieved.

Moreover, through compassion training it's possible not only to respond to suffering constructively, but also to prevent future suffering by recognizing the seeds of suffering that are being watered in the present. This preventive nature of compassion shows the link between compassion and wisdom, one aspect of which is the capacity to connect the invisible dots between causes and consequences.

Before going any deeper, let's explore how compassion can be evoked through a thought experiment. Since it's important to learn to offer ourselves what we would like to offer others, we'll begin with a self-compassion experiment. Remember to bring an open and curious attitude to the experiment and see what emerges in your own experience. There's no right or wrong way to do this experiment, nor any particular outcome to seek.

Experiment: Self-Compassion

Follow the instructions below, staying with each step for a few minutes before moving on to the next.

• Take a comfortable seated position and breathe deeply in and out a few times.

• Bring to mind an event or situation that is creating some difficulty or stress in your life. It could be something that didn't turn out as you expected, or perhaps something you regret having done or said that you criticize yourself for. Take a moment to feel whatever arises in relation to this event.

• Evoke the image or presence of someone who knows you deeply and accepts you with all your strengths and weaknesses. If it's difficult to think about someone concrete, bring to mind the image of someone you admire for his or her kindness and compassion, perhaps a spiritual guide or religious leader, or even an imaginary wise and loving being. Closing your eyes, imagine that person's presence as vividly as possible.

• Ask yourself: How would this person look at me? How would this person talk to me? What would he or she say? Take your time, and allow the words and emotions to emerge organically.

• Let yourself be soothed and held by the feelings of empathic concern, care, and friendliness that emerge from your compassionate friend.

• Bring one hand to your heart and feel your chest expanding and relaxing with each cycle of breath. Recognizing that the energy of the compassionate image is born out of the capacity for compassion in your own heart and mind, repeat this phrase silently a few times, letting it permeate your mind: "May I befriend myself. May I treat myself with love and compassion."

• For a moment, imagine all the people around the planet who are going through a similar difficult situation or pain, recognizing that your suffering doesn't isolate you but actually connects you with many other fellow human beings. From this widened perspective, imagine that the benefits of this self-compassion practice are also radiating to many others.

• Finally, see if you can recognize that, just like you, everyone else wishes to be seen and talked to with empathy, kindness, and compassion. If the following aspiration resonates with your core values, you can repeat it in your mind a few times: "May I offer this empathy and compassion to others."

• While you return to your breath, rest for a moment in the feeling of an open heart.

What did you notice? Write down whatever you observed in this experiment.

_____

You can turn this experiment into a regular self-compassion practice. This practice is especially useful when dealing with strong, difficult emotions, but it's always a good idea to practice self-compassion regularly, even when you feel okay about yourself. Each time you decide to practice, you strengthen the capacity to treat yourself with the empathy and compassion you deserve.

Self-Compassion and Compassion for Others

There's a deep connection between self-compassion and compassion for others. The Dalai Lama, one of the most enthusiastic promoters of compassion, says: "Loving oneself is crucial. If we do not love ourselves, how can we love others? It seems that when some people talk of compassion, they have the notion that it entails a total disregard for one's own interests—a sacrificing of one's interests. This is not the case. In fact, genuine love should first be directed at oneself" (Dalai Lama 1997, 143). This link shouldn't be too surprising, but it's actually a hard one to integrate into practice. Only when we slowly work on developing the habit of treating ourselves with kindness and compassion does this attitude begin to inform and shape the way we treat others.

The opposite is also true: If we have the habit of judging and criticizing ourselves harshly, it's just natural that we extend this judgmental habit toward others—overtly or not. In some way, you're one among many other characters on the stage of your mind, along with friends, colleagues, family members, and so on. All those characters are affected by the kind of conversation you hold inside your mind—the tone, the words, the pace, and the intention. How you talk to others outside your head tends to be a reflection of that inner dialogue.

Noticing the quality of the invisible conversation we hold with ourselves is a very interesting practice, and when people start paying attention to it during meditation, powerful insights may come. People begin to realize that they carry all sorts of borrowed or inherited self-criticisms, self-limiting beliefs, and harsh judgments. Many of them tend to come from a very young age, and some are vestiges of internalized voices of strict parents, severe teachers, cruel classmates, or competitive siblings. These voices tend to appear precisely when we're under pressure and feel most vulnerable, often acquiring the prominence of ultimate "truths," even if there's abundant objective data that contradicts them. It's like suffering from anorexia and still perceiving yourself as too fat.

Kristin Neff, a prominent self-compassion teacher and researcher, identifies three core components of self-compassion, but you can also think about these as components of compassion for others, since the main difference between the two is merely whether the object of compassion is yourself or others (Neff 2011). The first element is *kindness,* which involves taking an empathic and caring stance toward oneself when one feels inadequate, incompetent, or defective in some way. In the experiment above, kindness was evoked through imagining someone who deeply loved you and asking yourself: How would they look at you?

How would they talk to you? We tend to have a hard time offering ourselves the kindness, respect, and empathy we would offer to a dear friend in distress. The kindness component of self-compassion asks us: *Can you be your own friend when you most need it?*

The second element of self-compassion is *common humanity,* which involves resisting the tendency to isolate when you're under stress or feel down by thinking "This can only happen to me" ("I'm the only one who doesn't understand this," "I'm the only one who makes mistakes," "I'm the only boring person here," and so on). Instead, we practice remembering that we don't need to single ourselves out from the human race when things go awry, and even more fundamentally, that imperfection and pain are natural parts of the human experience. Our suffering isn't proof that something's fundamentally wrong with us, but proof that, just like anyone else in the world, we go through ups and downs. The common humanity aspect asks us: *Can you stay connected instead of isolating in this difficult moment?*

The third component is *mindfulness,* which, in this context, refers to the capacity to notice that suffering is present, and to observe it without becoming fully identified with or absorbed in it. In other words, it means being aware of suffering, but holding it in the wider embrace of awareness instead of shrinking our identity to the size of our particular suffering. The mindfulness aspect asks us: *Can you be fully present with this experience of suffering without forgetting that you're larger than it is?*

By bringing these aspects of self-compassion to your mind regularly, you can take a more balanced attitude toward difficult emotions, so that emotional pain isn't denied or repressed, and nor are you overidentifying with it. You're larger than your difficult emotions. Likewise for the suffering of others: you can turn toward it with care and concern, yet with a spacious and wise heart that doesn't drown in feelings of distress. Neff teaches a short mantra that can be used as a practical reminder of these three components. In a moment of distress, self-judgment, shame, preoccupation, or sadness you can practice bringing one hand to your chest, taking a couple of slow breaths, and repeating in your mind (or aloud, if you're comfortable doing so):

> *This is a moment of suffering.*
> *Suffering is part of life.*
> *May I be kind to myself in this moment.*
> *May I give myself the compassion I need.*

(Neff 2011, 119; reprinted with permission)

The first line of this short mantra invokes the mindfulness aspect; the second line invites the perspective of common humanity; and the last two lines are reminders of the kindness component. If you find this verse useful, try to memorize it, or write it down and put it somewhere you can easily read it.

Of course, you can also adjust the language to fit your own style. The important thing is that you charge the words with your intention, instead of just repeating them mechanically. Try this practice a few times and see what comes up in your own experience.

Common Humanity and Compassionate Perception

Recognizing our imperfections and fragility through the lens of self-compassion allows us to experience other people's shortcomings with more empathy and compassion. This is not only beneficial for us—because compassion for others lessens our own distress and reactivity toward others' imperfections—but it also offers other people the space to reconsider their attitudes rather than just becoming defensive. Awareness of our own fallibility can help us to pause for a moment before automatically judging others, trying instead to understand their situation and motivation better, from the perspective of common humanity. If we judge others too quickly from a place of self-righteousness, we run the risk of becoming arrogant and close-minded—an apparently solid but actually very fragile place to stand. In contrast, by acknowledging our own imperfections and learning to relate to them with gentleness and a good dose of humor, we can become humbler and warmer in our relationships with others.

Just as it's possible to be mindful of the ways we tend to judge ourselves, we can also become mindful of the ways we automatically judge, classify, and evaluate others. Considering how little we really know about others and their circumstances, it seems wise to cultivate a healthy dose of skepticism toward the judgments we create about them. Not only are these judgments a kind of toxic mental noise, but they're also usually untrue.

Social psychologists even talk about the "fundamental attribution error," a deeply ingrained bias that leads us to blame other people's behavior on their personal dispositions instead of considering their circumstances, while using the opposite logic when accounting for our own behavior: if my office is a mess it's because I was in a hurry, but if yours is a mess it's because *you're a messy person.* But the truth is that people (including us) have the incredibly persistent habit of being way more complex than our preconceptions about them.

The idea of suspending our fast judgments and offering the benefit of the doubt instead of jumping to conclusions doesn't mean we become blind or lily-livered in the face of people's hurtful actions. Referring back to the language of Nonviolent Communication (NVC; Rosenberg 2003) we can train ourselves to perceive unskillful actions (actions that lead to suffering) as "tragic expressions of unmet needs." What does this mean?

Consider this: Every action can be seen as an attempt to satisfy a particular basic human need. The strategy to meet that need may or may not be skillful, but the need itself deserves acknowledgment and respect. This perspective avoids merging the person with his actions, which means that we can strongly oppose the action while still relating to the person with empathy.

For example, imagine a teenager yelling at her mother something like: "Stop being so intrusive, stop manipulating my life! I want to make my own decisions! I hate you!" and then slamming the door in her mother's face. From a reactive stance we might be tempted to label the teenager as a "bad," "aggressive," or "impossible" kid, but this will not only sabotage the relationship, it will likely make the mother condemn herself for raising such a difficult child. This will then get communicated, directly or indirectly, to the daughter, feeding her feelings of low self-esteem. Instead, one could ask: "What is the legitimate human need behind this temper tantrum?" Here are some possible candidates: autonomy, self-worth, safety, respect. No doubt the teenager's behavior is unskillful—but it's actually a tragic expression of unmet needs. The "tragedy" lies in the fact that her very way of expressing her need makes it less likely that the need will actually be satisfied.

What would happen if we started seeing our own and other people's unskillful actions not as proof of how bad they are, but as "tragic expressions of unmet needs"?

Exercise: Perceiving Needs Behind Actions

Sit in a comfortable position and breathe deeply a couple of times. Bring to mind a situation where you did something that you criticize yourself for. It could be something that you said or did. Take your time to remember the situation in some detail and to notice the judgmental commentary that comes up when you think about that event.

Now, keeping the event in the back of your mind, take time to review the following list of basic human needs, and see whether you can identify one or more needs that could have driven your unskillful action or words. The idea is not to pretend the action was okay, but to explore the unmet needs that might have driven it. This list of basic human needs is taken from the work of Marshall Rosenberg (2003). It is not meant to be exhaustive; feel free to add needs that are not listed.

- **Autonomy:** To choose one's dreams, goals, values; to choose one's plan for fulfilling one's dreams, goals, values.

- **Integrity:** Authenticity; creativity; meaning; self-worth.

- **Interdependence:** Acceptance; appreciation; closeness; community; consideration; contribution to the enrichment of life; emotional safety; empathy; honesty; love; reassurance; support; understanding; warmth; cooperation.

- **Play:** Fun; laughter.

- **Spiritual Communion:** Beauty; harmony; inspiration; order; peace.

- **Physical Nurturance:** Air; food; movement/exercise; rest/sleep; sexual expression; safety; shelter; touch; water.

- **Respect, Safety, Trust**

Taking the following questions as cues for a sort of analytical meditation, reflect on them and see what comes up:

What might have been the basic need(s) behind the unskillful behavior?

What feelings arise when you recognize the unmet need(s) instead of getting stuck in the judgments about the action? (Let any feeling arise.) Is there a part of you that recognizes that the need was legitimate, even if the strategy to meet it wasn't the wisest?

_____

Can you think of alternative and more skillful strategies to meet the same need(s)?

_____

Would it be fair if someone defined and labeled you just from seeing this particular action? Does this action really define you? Would that label capture all the complexity of your being?

Once you're done, repeat the exercise considering someone else's unskillful action. For example, you can bring to mind something that a coworker, classmate, or dear one said or did that annoyed you or caused distress in your environment. Go through the list of basic needs again, keeping the event in mind, and then reflect on the questions above, this time using them as a meditation on empathy for others.

By reflecting on what we most need when we suffer, we can become aware of what others might need when *they* suffer. For example, from our own experience we know that when we suffer, we don't benefit from being judged or ridiculed; instead, we appreciate it if someone offers understanding, support, kindness, patience, and trust in our capacity to handle this suffering. Of course, simply *projecting* what we need onto others won't necessarily help them, and thus the perspective of shared, common humanity must be tempered and complemented with empathic accuracy—the capacity to accurately perceive the other person's feelings and needs. Thich Nhat Hanh speaks about the link between love and understanding in this way: "Without understanding, love is an impossible thing. What must we do in order to understand a person? We must have time; we must practice looking deeply into this person. We must be there, attentive; we must observe, we must look deeply. And the fruit of this looking deeply is called understanding. Love is a true thing if it is made up of a substance called understanding" (2004, 2–3).

To understand others, we need time to look deeply, and this is exactly what we do when we practice mindfulness. In the framework of cultivating compassion, mindfulness jumps off of the cushion and the practice becomes relational. Other people and their needs aren't distractions from practice; other people—with all their virtues and defects—are mindfulness bells that wake us up from distracted self-preoccupation. Ultimately, it's in our relationship with others where our practice gets real.

Practice Plan, Week 8

Meditation Practice: Compassion

(*recording available at* http://www.newharbinger.com /28395)

Find a place that is quiet and comfortable and position the body so you can be both relaxed and alert. Start with three deep, diaphragmatic breaths.

Now, bring to mind a compassionate image that represents the qualities of wisdom, strength, acceptance, love, nurturance, or caring. Imagine yourself in the presence of this source of compassion, the recipient of its great compassion. Feel how, in the presence of this compassionate image, you can be completely yourself—no need to impress anyone or to prove anything.

Now, think of a time in your life when you were suffering in some way. Notice how you feel when you remember this experience. Imagine seeing your own suffering through the eyes of your compassionate image.

With whatever feelings of warmth and caring you can call up for yourself, silently repeat these phrases, connecting as best you can with the feelings behind the words: "May I be free from this suffering. May I know peace and joy."

Now, bring to mind someone you care about, such as a family member or a friend, someone who naturally brings a smile to your face. Think of a time when this friend or loved one was suffering, noticing with gentle awareness how you feel as you bring this image to mind. Silently recite the following phrases, again doing your best to connect with the feelings behind the words: "May you be free from this suffering. May you know peace and joy."

Now, bring to mind someone you have no special sense of either closeness or conflict with; someone you would recognize, but don't really know. Consider the fact that, just like you, this person has had ups and downs in his or her life, this person has goals and dreams. Now imagine that this person is going through a time of great difficulty, perhaps financial stress, illness, or depression, and silently repeat these phrases: "May you be free from this suffering. May you know peace and joy."

Now, bring to mind a person you have some difficulty with. It might be someone with whom you don't get along, or someone you feel in competition with. Consider the fact that, just like you, this person has had ups and downs in his or her life. Imagine this person going through a time of difficulty and silently repeat these phrases: "May you be free from this suffering. May you know peace and joy."

Now, begin to expand the scope of your awareness from these three people to all the people who live on your street, in your neighborhood, and in the greater community, and silently repeat these phrases:

- May all beings be free from suffering.
- May all beings be free from sorrow.
- May all beings be free from fear.
- May all beings know peace and joy.

Finally, rest for a few moments in this state of open-hearted, open-minded compassion. Welcome the peace and happiness that this attitude of compassion may bring to your mind and body.

Compassion Practice—FAQs

- "I'm afraid that if I develop compassion toward myself, I'll become more self-indulgent."

  - Research has actually demonstrated the opposite: When you develop self-compassion, you have a better chance to meet your goals because you're less afraid of failing (you won't beat yourself up so hard), you're less prone to procrastinate (procrastination is linked to perfectionism), and you're more likely to reengage with your goals when you're off track (Neff 2011; Williams, Stark, and Foster 2008; Neff, Hsieh, and Dejitterat 2005).

- "Will I become more selfish and egocentric if I practice self-compassion?"

  - Self-compassionate people aren't more selfish. When you are nourished by a kind and empathic relation with yourself, you actually have more energy, attention, and compassion to offer others.

- "When I do the compassion meditation, I don't feel anything special. It's like I'm just repeating the words in my mind but nothing really happens."

  - What you train in compassion practice isn't a particular emotion, but familiarization with a particular mind-set and attitude. Remember that meditation means "cultivating" something (in this case, compassion). If you do the practice regularly, you'll notice that there will be days when you feel a lot and days when you feel nothing. This isn't important. The important thing is reconnecting over and over again with the intention to cultivate a compassionate attitude toward yourself and others.

- "This meditation is asking too much from me. I can feel compassion for my friends and family members, but compassion for strangers (let alone compassion for all humanity) feels too abstract and big."

    - This is a very common experience, especially when you are starting these practices. If compassion for strangers and all humanity seems too abstract at first, it's totally okay to stay with self-compassion and compassion for loved ones for a while. You can simply listen to the rest of the meditation instructions without really practicing, or you can even stop the recording at that point. After a few weeks of this practice, you can give the complete meditation a try again and see what happens. The mind-heart is flexible and dynamic; something that doesn't feel possible today may become your favorite practice later.

Practice Log
For each day that you do the compassion practice, fill in the following log. Keeping track of your insights

with the practices will help you integrate what you learn from your experiences over time.

Date and time	What stood out with this practice?

Field Observation: Recognizing Shared, Common Humanity

The following is a simple but effective practice to help you become more aware of your connection with other human beings: In your everyday life, when you encounter other people, simply observe them and take a moment to suspend any automatic opinions that come up. Reflect on these phrases: "Just like me, this person wants to be happy ... Just like me, this person wants to be free from suffering." As a shorthand version, you can bring to mind the phrase "Just like me."

Try this experiment in different contexts and with different people. You can practice this when you're around your partner or children, when you're at work or school, when you're with colleagues or classmates, or when you're shopping at the market. Invite a curious attitude toward this observation of others, and see if, in their gestures, behavior, routines, or even their irritating ways, you can catch a glimpse of their vulnerability, their genuine desire to be happy and to be free from suffering.

Without a specific goal in mind, observe what goes on within you and what happens in your interaction with others when you start looking at them from this perspective, when you begin training your perception to recognize our shared, common humanity.

Field Notes

_____

Field Observation: Writing a Self-Compassionate Letter

Bring to mind a recent difficult situation or something that is producing stress or suffering in your life. It can be a personal or relational problem, something that challenges your willpower, or some trouble you're having in trying to meet an important goal.

Write a compassionate letter to yourself about this experience from a second-person perspective, using the guidelines below. It's a good idea to write this letter after practicing mindful breathing or the compassion meditation. Include the following elements in your letter:

Mindfulness. Allow yourself to remember and think about your stress or suffering. In the letter, recognize and validate your emotions, thoughts, needs, and aspirations. For example: "Dear Amy, I know you're feeling sad/worried/fearful/etc. I know that you were trying/expecting/doing your best to..." Write about the specific stress or suffering, and also about the unmet need that this suffering is pointing to: autonomy, safety, celebration, space, connection, and so on (you can use the list from the "Perceiving Needs Behind Actions" exercise).

Common Humanity. Offer yourself a message of common humanity. For example: "Everybody sometimes feels that he or she has made a mistake/failed at something/gotten mad at someone else/experienced a loss/etc."

Kindness. Offer yourself compassionate advice or encouragement. You can try to imagine what you would say to a close friend in this situation. What would you say to someone you trust, love, and wish the best for?

After writing the compassionate letter, you can read it aloud to yourself or keep it for a while and pull it out when you need self-compassion. You could

> even put the letter in an envelope and mail it to yourself—it's very special to receive a compassionate letter from yourself in the mail.

Acknowledging that suffering is part of the fabric of life, in this chapter we've explored ways in which compassion can be a wise response to suffering that is conducive to long-term emotional balance. Since self-compassion and compassion for others are deeply connected, we proposed several practices to cultivate both. Ultimately, compassion makes our solidified sense of self become more porous and open, and through practice we begin to realize how the distinction between self-compassion and compassion for others is somewhat artificial. To really care for oneself *is* to care for others, and to care for others *is* really caring for oneself.

A key step in developing compassion is recognizing our shared, common humanity—seeing that, despite our differences, we're all together in this human boat. Mother Teresa of Calcutta once said: "The problem with the world is that we draw our family circle too small." No matter how similar to or different from other people we may feel, we can be certain that, *just like us,* everybody wants to enjoy good health, everybody wants love and respect, and everyone wants to live a meaningful life. We also know that, *just like us,* everybody wants to be free from suffering. When we recognize that even unskillful actions are expressions of unmet needs, we can develop kind eyes and skillful hands to respond in compassionate ways, even when dealing with difficult people. But remember: real compassion isn't soft and fuzzy; compassion may mean acting with strong determination and setting clear limits.

In these times, when suffering is evident on so many levels, compassion can be seen as a much-needed balm that can heal broken hearts, conflicted communities, and war-addicted nations. We hope this chapter is an open invitation for you to keep nourishing the seeds of compassion that are already in your heart.

Part 3

Sustaining and Deepening

Chapter 12

Diets of the Heart, Mind, and Body

SURFING THE FULL CATASTROPHE

Now that you've completed the eight-week program in Mindfulness-Based Emotional Balance, there's some good news and some bad news. The bad news (usually easier to hear first) is that you will continue to suffer and experience emotional turmoil as long as you're alive and conscious. The good news is that you now have the tools to recover your equilibrium more quickly and to transform the unavoidable suffering of life—"the full catastrophe"—into wisdom and compassion. Better still, the moment suffering is met with mindfulness it is lessened, and there's often joy in knowing that you're able to surf even the rogue waves of emotion that might have threatened to engulf you before this training.

Before moving on to consider how to apply what you've learned to your daily life, let's take a few minutes to reflect on what has stood out for you from the array of exercises and practices you've been working with.

Exercise: What Have I Learned?

This is a guided visualization exercise in which you will reflect on what you've learned over the past eight weeks—or eight chapters—of this book. Try not to do this exercise in a rush, but to allow enough space before and after the main part of the exercise to practice mindfulness of breathing. The intention here is to consolidate what you've learned through reflection and writing.

Use the following instructions as a guide, modifying them as you need to. Please read each bullet point and then take two or three minutes to follow the instructions before moving to the next bullet.

• Sit in meditation posture, in a comfortable yet alert position, with your hands resting comfortably and your eyes gently closed. Check in with the body, feeling the places where it makes contact with the chair or floor.

• Take some deep breaths, completely filling the torso with air, then completely releasing the breath.

• Now, imagine that you could look at your engagement with this workbook from the perspective of a bird, soaring over the landscape. As you fly, you can see the prominent features of the ground beneath you. Now, imagine that on the ground below you can see the practices, exercises, and experiments that were offered in this workbook. Which ones stand out to you? What have you been able to use? What has contributed to your emotional balance? Take as much time as you need to review both what you've learned and how it has impacted your life.

After you finish, take a few minutes to write down whatever you'd like to remember from this visualization.

Notes

_____

The Problem with Diets

There are at least two problems with diets. The first is that they usually don't work, and the second is that they focus only on food. In fact, the second problem may explain the first problem, at least in part. Let's explore the second problem and then circle back to the unfortunate fact that diets—when understood as a food plan to lose weight—generally don't work in the long term. Traci Mann and her colleagues at the University of California, Los Angeles analyzed thirty-one long-term studies on dieting and found that the majority of people who lost weight gained the same amount back and more (Mann et al. 2007).

When most people hear the word "diet," they don't typically think of Internet surfing, texting, TV, music, or conversations. Diets usually conjure up images of unappealing food served in small portions. But it could be argued that our senses are being fed by stimulation, just as our bodies are being fed by the food we eat. The diets of our senses are processed in our brains, and give rise to the thoughts we think. And research on neuroplasticity is revealing that our brains are constantly being shaped by our thoughts.

This might seem obvious when you read it on the page, yet our habits are often hidden from the plain light of logic. For example, many people have trouble sleeping at night. Sleep researchers say that exhaustion has reached epic proportions. In 2003 it was estimated that "50 to 70 million Americans chronically suffer from a disorder of sleep and wakefulness, hindering daily functioning and adversely affecting health and longevity" (NHLBI 2003). How many of these people watch news on TV before they go to sleep? How many have their laptops in bed? How many of them have an argument late at night with their partners, or watch a television show that elevates their heart rate? We'll never know for sure, but these are pretty common scenarios.

The diets of our bodies mainly involve the food we eat, but it could be argued that everything we do to sustain the body is, in some sense, a diet. The word diet does come, after all, from the Greek word (diaita), which means "a way of life." So this wider interpretation might include exercise, hygiene, medical attention, sunscreen, moisturizers, rest, sex, touch, and so on, as well as all the foods and liquids we consume. What, then, is the relationship between the body's diet and emotional balance?

Experiment: Connecting the Dots

Hopefully, by now you are enjoying the process of using your own life and experience as a laboratory in which to understand how to develop greater happiness and emotional balance. In order to look beyond the cunning rationalizations of habit, you will need the unblinking steadiness of the researcher's gaze. Beginning now, and then continuing indefinitely (or as long as it's useful), reflect on the habits, or diets, of the body that negatively impact your emotional balance. Use the space below to begin to connect the dots between how you feed the body, in the broadest sense, and how you feel.

Notes

As suggested in the first paragraph of this section, we believe that one reason diets often don't work is because both overeating and consuming calorie-laden comfort foods are often due to emotional imbalance.

Sadly, when emotional discomfort arises, most people engage in an activity that will only serve to increase their distress and send them on a downward spiral involving the "usual suspects" of shame, agitation, self-criticism, withdrawal, avoidance, and so on. Or, as the great meditation teacher Ajahn Chah succinctly put it: "To run from suffering is to run toward it."

Connecting the dots, not only between diets of the senses and emotional balance, but between distressing emotions and patterns of avoidance, reveals the essentially circular nature of experience. Fortunately, it's possible to intervene with mindfulness and wisdom at any point in this circle.

In chapter 3 we explored intention as the invisible force that drives the outcome of our actions, and investigated its relationship to emotional balance. Another often-neglected yet powerful time to pay special care to intention is before eating. Whether we're dieting or indulging, what is the intention that's driving our behavior? If diet—or even exercise—is motivated by self-punishment rather than self-care, how does this intention impact the outcome? By bringing awareness to our intentions, it's possible to intervene *before* beginning the downward spiral described above. The biggest field experiment of them all, the mother of all field experiments, is noticing the connection between your intentions, your actions, and your state of mind.

Ethics and Emotional Balance

Though ethics and morality have historically been under the purview of religion, the Dalai Lama has been a staunch and compelling advocate of secular ethics. In his book *Ethics for the New Millennium,* he presents a moral framework based on universal rather than religious principles. It rests on the observation that those whose conduct is ethically positive are happier and more satisfied, and the belief that much of the unhappiness we endure is actually of our own making. In short, ethical behavior is the basis for emotional balance.

When meditation is taught in a monastery, even lay practitioners are required to follow a set of precepts (such as not harming, not stealing, refraining from misconduct, and so on) that serve several functions. Naturally, they create a more harmonious living environment. Equally important, however, is their power to quiet the mind. In the Theravada tradition, from which most mindfulness-based interventions derive, the principal aim of meditation practice is to liberate the mind from greed, hatred, and delusion. In order for the mind to realize the insights that give rise to this freedom, it must get quiet and still enough to see beyond, or beneath, the habitual ways that we perceive reality. And the more ethical our behavior, the quieter the mind.

The Dalai Lama is also famous for saying, "If you want to be happy, practice compassion. If you want others to be happy, practice compassion." In this way, he's linking happiness with ethical behavior. From a Buddhist perspective, true happiness arises not out of sense satisfaction or material acquisition, but from a mind that's able to perceive the nature of reality. From this clear seeing, compassion, kindness, and emotional balance naturally arise.

Although many moral precepts take the form of "Thou shalt not...," they can just as easily be articulated in a positive manner. It is unethical to be cruel to those who suffer, just as it is ethical to be compassionate to those who suffer. For many people, there's automatic resistance to anything that's heard as a demand. As soon as the word "should" enters the conversation, even if we're only speaking to ourselves, a weariness, unwillingness, or downright rebellion rears up, and that "should" becomes the last thing in the world we want to do. Our colleague Kelly McGonigal writes about this beautifully in her book *The Science of Willpower* (2012). Have you noticed how the shoulds pile up? It's like we're carrying around an invisible backpack of all the things we should be doing, or should've done.

In two academic papers on mindfulness, Margaret (Cullen 2011) and Gonzalo (Brito 2014) wrote about how mindfulness-based interventions (MBIs) can promote secular, rather than religious, ethics, and how the inclusion of ethics and intentions brings a deeper and broader context to mindfulness, so that we don't mistake it for the latest stress-management technique. This is appropriate because MBIs are typically taught in mainstream settings to participants with a wide range of beliefs and "nonbeliefs." In this workbook, you're being invited to go one step further and take responsibility for your own personal ethics, not because you *should,* but because it will lead to your own happiness and emotional balance. In turn, it will benefit all those you come in contact with.

Exercise: Write Your Precepts

Before you begin, take a moment to review what you wrote in response to the "Three Questions" guided visualization in chapter 3. In fact, feel free to listen again to that visualization and see if your answers have changed or stayed the same.

When you're ready, take a moment to reflect on what precepts you would like to undertake that will support your greatest happiness and emotional balance. Notice any tendencies to use this exercise as just another way to beat yourself up, or "should" yourself, and see if you can choose, instead, a motivation of self-care and self-compassion. Some examples of precepts include: not taking that which isn't freely offered; telling the truth; refraining from sexual behavior that leads to one's own or another's suffering; not harming oneself or others; speaking with kindness; and practicing generosity.

Before you begin writing, consider how realistic these precepts are for your life as it is right now. What do you feel happy about undertaking? What time frame is realistic for you? Would you like to try these precepts for a day? For a week? This is a serious agreement, not because you'll be struck by lightning if you fail to deliver, but because you will have disappointed *yourself* and added more weight to the invisible backpack of all the things you should be doing, or didn't do well enough.

Notes

_____

In this chapter, we've circled back to part 1, specifically revisiting intention, and begun to explore approaching all of life as practice. The wonderful thing about this word "practice" is that it suggests a work in progress, a process of becoming, rather than a static ideal. We widened the definition of "diet" to include everything you take in with all your senses, and to connect the dots between your experiences or actions and your emotional balance.

It's helpful to revisit, again and again, what really matters to you—your personal values—and then to don your lab coat in the biggest experiment of them all, that of your life. See if you can look directly, unflinchingly, and yet kindly at the relationship between cause and effect. You alone are the expert on this, you are the Principal Investigator, the priest, the rabbi, the Einstein, the Nobel laureate. Only *you* can really know how it feels in your mind and body when you do call your mother or when you don't call your mother. It's our premise that ethics, when derived in this deeply personal way, have the greatest potential for enduring and for increasingly informing all of our actions.

It's helpful to remember, too, that however noble your intentions, you'll never be perfect. When you're tired or particularly stressed, you're more likely to violate your own precepts. When this happens—*and it will*—forgiveness and self-compassion are the keys to regaining emotional balance. And it's just this self-forgiveness that will allow you to be kinder and more forgiving with others. In such moments, it can also be humbling to witness the power of habit, how quickly it can usurp the new behaviors you have learned in this book. Know that this is common, and it's not your fault! Take comfort in knowing that whatever led you to this book, to these practices, and to your own deepest values, is like a North Star—both guiding you and unreachable at the same time.

Chapter 13

Continuation of Practice

RESISTANCE AND FORWARD MOMENTUM

From our own experience with the practices we offer in this book, and also from accompanying the practices of hundreds of others, we know that the path of cultivating mindfulness and emotional balance is not a straight line of steady progress. Actually, it's closer to an intricate curvy road with many ups and downs, detours, and all sorts of unexpected adventures—like life itself. Because the core aspects of this program are more experiential than intellectual, simply getting the main ideas right won't substitute for the long-term effort (and benefits) of regular practice. The end of a program or book like this isn't "...and she lived mindfully ever after."

Without establishing regularity in your practice, its benefits aren't likely to last for long, because mental and emotional habits that have been cultivated over decades will naturally take over again. It's like tending a garden—you can't just water and weed once a year and hope for the best. Even if the gardener loves her work, for a garden to thrive this love and interest must be complemented with a certain degree of discipline. The work of gardening can't depend just on the gardener's mood. Meditation teacher Ajahn Sumedho once said: "Our practice is not to follow the heart; it is to train the heart" (cited in Goldstein 2007, 71). Although the *motto* "Follow your heart" might sound appealing, it does not take into account the fact that the heart could have some problematic habit energies. To cultivate a healthy mind and an open heart, we can't simply do what we feel like—the heart's voice must be tempered by discerning wisdom and appropriate effort.

Interestingly, even if we have an experiential taste of the benefits of practice, it's rarely an easy endeavor to establish a regular practice routine. Many outer obstacles and inner resistances commonly arise: "I have too little time," "I have too much work to do," "I'm too tired," "Others need me," "I don't have a quiet place to practice," "I can't do it right," "It's too cold," "It's too hot," "I don't have the right bell/incense/yoga pants/cushion/timer/app" ... We can come up with endless reasons *not* to practice. We (Margaret and Gonzalo) have yet to hear of a single person—including prominent meditation teachers—who hasn't gone through ups and downs in his practice life; and we ourselves have certainly gone through periods of less intense practice and even no practice at all, and times when practice has seemed fruitless, dry, and unproductive. Going through these phases is another aspect of our shared, common humanity.

At those times, it's important to remember that even resistance and obstacles aren't outside the scope of practice. In the same way that mental distractions aren't really obstacles in our sitting, in the bigger picture of real-life practice the obstacles we encounter are part of the path. Actually, the obstacles reveal the path because they highlight our "edges"—the places that are calling for further exploration and development, and where growth is possible.

Although it's impossible not to have obstacles on one's path, it's always possible to transform them into opportunities for practice. Practice is a lens through which you can choose to look at your life. Remember that, in a broader sense, you're always practicing something (you always have a lens through which you approach life), so it's more a matter of *what* you're practicing rather than *if* you're practicing. From this perspective, every situation is an opportunity for practice, and everyone we meet is a teacher.

Approaching our obstacles as the path itself, we can cultivate mindfulness, forgiveness, and compassion toward our very resistance to practice mindfulness, forgiveness, and compassion. This is a kind of metapractice: no matter where you are and how you feel about your practice—whether it's enthusiasm, boredom, bliss, sleepiness, interest, and so on—you can always go back to the basic intention and values that brought you to these practices (see chapters 3 and 12) and ask yourself: What would it mean to invite mindfulness and compassion right into this situation, right into this moment?

We'd like to share some strategies to help you leverage whatever forward momentum and inspiration you've gained from working with this book to navigate the obstacles and resistance that will naturally arise. But let's first take a moment to explore your own potential challenges and resistance, as well as your resources for maintaining a regular practice. Foreseeing potential obstacles takes away the "surprise factor," helping us to come up with creative ways to preempt them or to deal with them effectively. Also, our suggestions will make more sense after you have a clearer idea of your specific situation.

Exercise: Identifying Obstacles, Resistance, and Resources

In this exercise, you will reflect on what might come up for you as obstacles or resistance to establishing or maintaining a regular practice, as well as some potential resources to help you cope with them. The intention here is to use reflection and writing to identify the "usual suspects" that can get in your way. Use the following instructions as a guide, modifying them as you need to. Start this exercise with a brief centering practice, and then take a couple of minutes with each step before moving on to the next one.

• Sit in meditation posture, in a comfortable yet alert position, with your hands resting comfortably and your eyes gently closed. Check in with the body, feeling the places where it makes contact with the chair or floor. Take some deep breaths, completely filling the torso with air, then completely release the breath.

• Now, in your mind's eye, picture your daily life. How are your days and weeks structured? Think of your schedule, habits, and daily routines.

• Imagine yourself establishing a daily meditation practice. What would that look like? Reflect on the ways you could create space for practice, trying to be as concrete and realistic as you can. Write down any ideas that come to mind.

_____

• Now, think for a moment about inner resistances and outer obstacles that could get in the way of practice. Write them down.

_____

• Finally, reflect on inner and outer resources that could help you prevent or deal effectively with the obstacles and resistances you listed above.

_____

Read your responses and see if there's anything else you would like to add. Looking at potential resistances, obstacles, and resources, see if you get a clearer picture of how it would look to establish a regular practice.

Establishing a Regular Practice

Now that you have a clearer sense of your own situation in regard to practice, we would like to share some guidelines that many others have found useful. These aren't universal truths (one size doesn't fit all), but general guidelines that you can try out to see if they make sense in your own experience. First we'll propose some general principles, and then we'll get to more specific suggestions.

Set realistic expectations. Unrealistic expectations naturally create inner resistance to practice. When you decide to establish a practice routine, be realistic about what you can and can't do. For instance, if you get home from work at 9:00p.m. and you're planning to do your practice at 11:00p.m. (when the kids are asleep, finally), it's very likely that you'll also fall asleep as soon as you sit on the meditation cushion. Similarly, planning to start waking up at 3:30a.m. because you read somewhere that the Dalai Lama does his first practice at that time of the day can be a bad idea. It's preferable to commit to a sustainable pace of fewer and shorter regular practice sessions at a realistic time rather than an intense practice schedule that would require major adjustments in your life or in other people's lives.

Celebrate small victories. Our brains and minds have a tendency to focus on what's wrong and what doesn't work. This is why it's especially important to purposefully pay attention to what does work in your practice, and to take some time to savor the pleasure of small victories. For example, it's important to notice and celebrate any moment when emotional distress doesn't escalate to panic; when you can identify a self-deprecating thought as "just another thought"; when you choose forgiveness instead of holding on to resentment; or when you take some time off to cool down instead of escalating aggression into a heated argument. Small victories are important because it's in the smaller, apparently insignificant instances where long-term transformation takes place.

Identify inner resistances. As we have discussed throughout this program, there's an important link between resistance to present-moment experience and emotional distress. Difficult emotions feed on our reluctance to accept and relate to what's happening inside and outside. Therefore, a general guideline for daily practice is to be mindful of situations, people, emotions, and thoughts that evoke resistance, and explore the possibility of responding in new ways, instead of just reacting. Training yourself to turn toward rather than run away from what triggers resistance can be a powerful daily practice in itself.

See relationships as a field of practice. As human beings, we exist in relationship and interdependence, and our emotional lives influence and are influenced by the way we relate to others. Zen teacher Charlotte Joko Beck referred to the importance of relationships as a field of practice in these terms: "As we endeavor to practice with relationships, we begin to see that they are our best way to grow. In them we can see what our mind, our body, our senses, and our thoughts really are. Why are relationships such excellent practice? ... Because, aside from our formal sitting, there is no way that is superior to relationships in helping us see where we're stuck and what we're holding on to. As long as our buttons are pushed, we have a great chance to learn and grow. So a relationship is a great gift, not because it makes us happy—it often doesn't—but because any intimate relationship, if we view it as practice, is the clearest mirror we can find" (1989, 88–89). The suggestion, then, is to broaden the view of practice beyond a purely individual perspective and to pay attention to the myriad ways in which core elements of practice (attention, awareness, equanimity, empathy, compassion) can be trained in the way you relate to others.

Create a place for practice. It's very helpful to find or create a quiet corner at home and keep it as a place that's ready to be used for meditation practice. You don't need a whole room, or a fancy place—even a 3'x4' corner in a room might be enough. If you have a meditation-ready space, you don't have to set things up each time. In this space you can place a meditation cushion (or a chair, if you prefer), along with some books (such as this one), inspiring images, and even flowers, incense, a stone, or anything else that evokes the qualities you will cultivate in this place. None of these objects are necessary, but they can help you create an inspiring place where you want to spend some time.

Choose a time that works for you. Although people vary in their preferences and predispositions, it's usually a good idea to establish a regular time for meditation practice, instead of having to decide each time when to practice. It doesn't really matter if you practice early in the morning, late in the evening, or sometime in between. The idea is not to wait for the "perfect moment"—it doesn't exist—or to feel a strong desire or need to practice, but to do it regularly, as you would any other wholesome habit, like brushing your teeth. Many people find, however, that it's easier to meditate first thing in the morning: The mind is brighter, better rested, and less agitated. We strongly discourage "binge meditation"—if you didn't meditate at all the whole week, don't try to catch up by sitting for five hours on Sunday. This is like being sedentary all week and then working out at the gym for five hours straight on Saturday. Physical and mental training are similar in this sense—there's a tipping point after which further effort does more harm than good.

Start with shorter sits. It's usually better to start with short but regular periods of practice, perhaps ten or fifteen minutes, and then gradually increase the duration of your sitting meditations until you reach twenty-five or thirty minutes, or longer. Even when you're using the guided meditations, you can simply pause the recording and take a break if you need to. As a general rule, it's better to end the sitting when you're still enthusiastic about it, rather than finish with the feeling that you just barely managed to survive the sit. Although some meditators get caught up in competing for who's able to sit still the longest, the truth is that meditation is not a quantitative business—what really matters is the quality of your time on the cushion.

Decide what you're going to practice in advance. Deciding which practice you'll do right when you sit down to meditate can be confusing and wearing in the long run—the mind seems to benefit from a certain structure and predictability. In this book, we suggested that you maintain the same practice for a week before moving on to the next one. Now that you've finished the program, you can go over the same eight-week cycle again and again, or you can stay with the same practice for longer than a week. Each chapter's topic is juicy enough to keep us busy for a long time, so don't hesitate if you want to stay, for example, with the forgiveness practice for a month or two. Having said this, it's also perfectly okay if on any given day you really feel you would benefit from doing a different practice. Trust your own discernment. However, once you begin the practice, don't "fast forward" to another one, because this tends to reinforce *inattention* rather than strengthening *attention.*

Keep in mind the core elements of the program. Although you've learned a broad variety of practices in this book, it's good to keep in mind the core aspects of the program so that you can evoke them and use them whenever you need to—breath awareness; awareness of feelings, thoughts, and emotions; forgiveness; choosing kindness and compassion for self and others. A simple way to keep these core practices alive and relevant is to set your intentions for the day—for example, the intention to cultivate a stable mind and an open heart—and do a nightly check-in about it, taking some time to appreciate any moments when you were able to embody your morning intention.

Use informal practice as wedges of wisdom and compassion in daily life. You can use the experiments and field observations from this book as "informal practices"—practices off the meditation cushion. The idea is to turn your practice for emotional balance into a way of life, informing how you relate to yourself and others.

Use a meditation diary (or an app). It can be useful to have a meditation diary in addition to, or instead of, the practice logs that you used in part 2 of this book. The idea is not to interrupt your practice to write down some great ideas that came up while you were meditating, but to write a few notes afterward about what was salient for you in your practice. Keeping track of your practice in this way not only provides a valuable record of your process, but also helps you anchor and integrate the insights you gain and bring them to your life off the cushion. Nowadays there's also the more techy option of using a smartphone app. Some apps have various functions, including meditation timer, meditation diary, statistics on meditation time, and connecting with a large online community.

Connect with community and other resources. Meeting with a few people or a group to do meditation practice together is a powerful way to keep your motivation strong and to hold yourself accountable for your practice. Besides the resources we provide in the back of this book, it's a good idea to look for local sitting groups, meditation classes, or interesting talks related to these topics. Even if the group practices aren't identical to the ones you've learned in this program, it's very likely that you'll still benefit from the group support and energy. Besides attending classes, retreats, and sitting groups, you can also nourish your practice through reading books, magazines, and journal articles about meditation. See the "Additional Resources" section at the end of the book for things we've found useful.

We hope you find these suggestions helpful in establishing a regular practice, because there's no real substitute for regular practice to train your mind and heart. Mental and emotional fitness, just like physical fitness, requires regularity and effort—not the kind of effort that makes you clench your teeth and get all stressed out, but a kind effort motivated by self-respect and your legitimate wish to live a good life.

Just like the rest of life, practice is a constantly unfolding process that changes all the time. As you keep paying attention to this subtle aspect of life, you'll start recognizing new dimensions and angles, like new branches growing from a tree. If you get distracted or lack discipline and end up not practicing as much as you had expected to, don't beat yourself up—this only creates additional resistance. Pay attention to the organic process unfolding inside of you instead of obsessing about having the perfect conditions or doing it right. Even if you practice a little bit, you'll gradually reach your goals. A large container is filled drop by drop.

Conclusion

Conclusions are never easy, in part because they are somewhat artificial. All of life is a process, and beginnings and endings are intimately intertwined. As we said in chapter 1, the path to emotional balance, wholeness, and integration is nonlinear, and there's no endpoint either. While writing this conclusion, Margaret found herself knocked off balance by an upsetting email and Gonzalo found himself surfing the waves of anxiety having a loved one at the hospital. Both of us found solace in reviewing these pages and reminding ourselves of what we already deeply knew to be true, but forgot in moments of intense emotion.

In many ways, the job of this workbook is to remind you of what you already know, and lead you back to who you already are. Most of us need lots of reminders. It's so easy to forget. Good friends can help with this, as can all the suggestions in the last chapter. And there's no shame in going back to the beginning and just starting over, again and again.

The beauty of mindfulness is just this possibility of starting over, right here and right now. Whatever happened last year, last week, or in response to an email five minutes ago is over. And complete unconditional redemption is possible in any moment of unadulterated awareness. Emotions happen, angry words emerge bafflingly from our mouths like rabbits from a magician's hat, and the person we adored five minutes ago has suddenly grown horns and can do no right.

Emotion theorists like Paul Ekman assure us that this is what it's like to be a sentient being. Emotions are an exquisite part of being human, and they can be understood. They have causes and functions, and they behave in somewhat predictable ways. This intellectual understanding, as outlined in the chapters on emotion, anger, and fear, can help to normalize emotions, make them more "user friendly" and less threatening. It helps to know that, when you're in a refractory period of fear, everything looks more menacing and dangerous.

Mindfulness is that which allows us to recognize the refractory period when it's happening, and that which creates the space in the mind enabling us to identify the distorted perceptions that are caused by the refractory period. Mindfulness is the key that unlocks the power of these intellectual understandings and allows us to deploy them where the rubber meets the road: right in the middle (or, more likely, a few minutes later!) of the upsetting email, health crisis, or intense conversation with your partner. In a moment of true mindfulness, there's not only awareness, but also forgiveness and love. Whatever is arising can be met with unconditional acceptance. This love transcends individual desire and attachment and leads us directly into a dimension of ourselves that goes beyond our personal stories, giving us immediate access to the unlimited wellspring of kindness and compassion within.

Through the practices of kindness and compassion cultivation, the heart becomes suppler, and suppleness is the source of resilience. That which was frozen begins to thaw, the hard edges start to soften, the closed doors of the heart open. Perhaps most importantly, we see that we're not alone. These practices remind us of our shared, common humanity, and this awareness not only soothes our own pain and sorrow, but brings us closer to others.

Though we may not have met personally, we are all in this together. Thank you for walking this path with us. The anticipation of your interest in Mindfulness-Based Emotional Balance has allowed us to delve deeply into subjects we care profoundly about. We write to ourselves as much as we write to you. In this way, we are all walking each other home.

Additional Resources

Books

Brach, T. 2003. *Radical Acceptance: Embracing Your Life with the Heart of a Buddha.* New York: Bantam Books.

Chödrön, P. 1991. *The Wisdom of No Escape: And the Path of Loving-Kindness.* Boston: Shambhala.

Chödrön, P. 2000. *When Things Fall Apart: Heart Advice for Difficult Times.* Boston: Shambhala.

Chödrön, P. 2001. *Start Where You Are: A Guide to Compassionate Living.* Boston: Shambhala.

Dalai Lama. 1999. *Ethics for the New Millennium.* New York: Riverhead Books.

Dalai Lama. 2001. *The Compassionate Life.* Boston: Wisdom Publications.

Dalai Lama. 2002. *How to Practice: The Way to a Meaningful Life.* New York: Pocket Books.

Dalai Lama and H.C. Cutler. 2009. *The Art of Happiness in a Troubled World.* London: Hodder and Stoughton.

De Waal, F.B.M. 2009. *The Age of Empathy: Nature's Lessons for a Kinder Society.* New York: Harmony Books.

Ekman, P. 2008. *Emotional Awareness: Overcoming the Obstacles to Psychological Balance and Compassion: A Conversation Between the Dalai Lama and Paul Ekman.* New York: Times Books.

Feldman, C. 2005. *Compassion: Listening to the Cries of the World.* Berkeley, CA: Rodmell Press.

Germer, C.K., and R.D. Siegel. 2012. *Wisdom and Compassion in Psychotherapy: Deepening Mindfulness in Clinical Practice.* New York: Guilford Press.

Gilbert, P., and Choden. 2013. *Mindful Compassion.* London: Robinson.

Goldstein, J. 1994. *Insight Meditation: The Practice of Freedom.* Boston: Shambhala.

Goleman, D. 2003. *Destructive Emotions: How Can We Overcome Them?: A Scientific Dialogue with the Dalai Lama.* New York: Bantam.

Gunaratana, H. 2002. *Mindfulness in Plain English.* Boston: Wisdom Publications.

Hanson, R. 2013. *Hardwiring Happiness: The New Brain Science of Contentment, Calm, and Confidence.* New York: Random House.

Jinpa, T. 2011. *Essential Mind Training: Tibetan Wisdom for Daily Life.* Boston: Wisdom Publications.

Kabat-Zinn, J. 1994. *Wherever You Go, There You Are: Mindfulness in Everyday Life.* New York: Hyperion.

Kabat-Zinn, J. 2013. *Full Catastrophe Living: Using the Wisdom of Your Body and Mind to Face Stress, Pain, and Illness.* Rev. ed. New York: Bantam.

Khema, A. 2001. *Being Nobody, Going Nowhere: Meditations on the Buddhist Path.* Boston: Wisdom Publications.

Kornfield, J. 1994. *A Path with Heart.* New York: Bantam.

Kornfield, J. 2002. *The Art of Forgiveness, Lovingkindness, and Peace.* New York: Bantam.

Loizzo, J. 2012. *Sustainable Happiness: The Mind Science of Well-Being, Altruism, and Inspiration.* New York: Routledge.

Luskin, F. 2002. *Forgive for Good: A Proven Prescription for Health and Happiness.* San Francisco: Harper-Collins.

McKay, M., P. Fanning, and P.Z. Ona. 2011. *Mind and Emotions: A Universal Treatment for Emotional Disorders.* Oakland, CA: New Harbinger Publications.

Nguyen, A.H., and Thich Nhat Hanh. 2006. *Walking Meditation.* Boulder, CO: Sounds True.

Salzberg, S. 1995. *Lovingkindness: The Revolutionary Art of Happiness.* Boston: Shambhala.

Salzberg, S., and R.A.F. Thurman. 2013. *Love Your Enemies: How to Break the Anger Habit and Be a Whole Lot Happier.* Carlsbad, CA: Hay House.

Segal, Z.V., J.M.G. Williams, and J.D. Teasdale. 2002. *Mindfulness-Based Cognitive Therapy for Depression: A New Approach to Preventing Relapse.* New York: Guilford Press.

Tsering, T., T. Zopa, and G. McDougall. 2006. *Buddhist Psychology.* Boston: Wisdom Publications.

Wallace, B.A. 2001. *Buddhism with an Attitude: The Tibetan Seven-Point Mind-Training.* Ithaca, NY: Snow Lion Publications.

Wallace, B.A. 2006. *The Attention Revolution: Unlocking the Power of the Focused Mind.* Boston: Wisdom Publications.

Websites

Center for Compassion and Altruism Research and Education http://ccare.stanford.edu
Center for Mindfulness http://www.umassmed.edu/cfm

Center for Mindful Self-Compassion http://www.cente
rformsc.org

Compassionate Mind Foundation http://www.compassi
onatemind.co.uk

Greater Good Science Center http://www.greatergood
.berkeley.edu

Mind and Life Institute http://www.mindandlife.org

Paul Ekman Group (Paul Ekman's site) http://www.pa
ulekman.com

Self-Compassion (Kristin Neff's site) http://www.self-c
ompassion.org

UCLA Mindful Awareness Research Center http://www
.marc.ucla.edu

Audio Resources

Buddhist Geeks Podcast http://www.buddhistgeeks.co
m/category/podcast

Dharma Seed http://www.dharmaseed.org

Sounds True http://www.soundstrue.com

Magazines

Inquiring Mind http://www.inquiringmind.com

Mindful http://www.mindful.org/mindful-magazine

Shambhala Sun http://www.lionsroar.com

Tricycle http://www.tricycle.com

Meditation and Retreat Centers

East Bay Meditation Center (EBMC), Oakland, California
http://www.eastbaymeditation.org

Insight Meditation Society, Barre, Massachusetts http
://www.dharma.org

Omega Institute, Rhinebeck, New York http://www.eo
mega.org

Spirit Rock Meditation Center, Woodacre, California h
ttp://www.spiritrock.org

References

Abuelaish, I. 2011. *I Shall Not Hate: A Gaza Doctor's Journey on the Road to Peace and Human Dignity.* New York: Walker and Co.

Barbery, M. 2008. *The Elegance of the Hedgehog.* Translated by A. Anderson. New York: Europa Editions.

Bartlett, M., and D. DeSteno. 2006. "Gratitude and Prosocial Behavior: Helping When It Costs You." *Psychological Science* 17: 319–25.

Beck, C.J., and S. Smith. 1989. *Everyday Zen: Love and Work.* San Francisco: HarperCollins.

Benn, R., T. Akiva, S. Arel, and R.W. Roeser. 2012. "Mindfulness Training Effects for Parents and Educators of Children with Special Needs." *Developmental Psychology* 48: 1476–87.

Brito, G. 2014. "Rethinking Mindfulness in the Therapeutic Relationship." *Mindfulness* 5: 351–59.

Carson, J.W., F.J. Keefe, V. Goli, A.M. Fras, T.R. Lynch, S.R. Thorp, and J.L. Buechler. 2005. "Forgiveness and Chronic Low Back Pain: A Preliminary Study Examining the Relationship of

Forgiveness to Pain, Anger, and Psychological Distress." *Journal of Pain* 6: 84–91.

Correll, J., S.J. Spencer, and M.P. Zanna. 2004. "An Affirmed Self and an Open Mind: Self-Affirmation and Sensitivity to Argument Strength." *Journal of Experimental Social Psychology* 40: 350–56.

Creswell, J.D., W.T. Welch, S.E. Taylor, D.K. Sherman, T.L. Gruenewald, and T. Mann. 2005. "Affirmation of Personal Values Buffers Neuroendocrine and Psychological Stress Responses." *Psychological Science* 16: 846–51.

Cullen, M. 2011. "Mindfulness-Based Interventions: An Emerging Phenomenon." *Mindfulness* 2: 186–93.

Cullen, M., and R. Kabatznick. 2004. "The Traveling Peacemaker: A Conversation with Marshall Rosenberg." *Inquiring Mind* 21: 4–7.

Dalai Lama. 1997. *The Four Noble Truths: Fundamentals of Buddhist Teachings.* London: Thorsons.

Ekman, P. 2003. *Emotions Revealed: Recognizing Faces and Feelings to Improve Communication and Emotional Life.* New York: Times Books.

Emmons, R.A., and M.E. McCullough. 2003. "Counting Blessings versus Burdens: An Experimental Investigation of Gratitude and Subjective Well-Being

284

in Daily Life." *Journal of Personality and Social Psychology* 84: 377–89.

Fredrickson, B. 2014. *Love 2.0: Creating Happiness and Health in Moments of Connection.* New York: Plume.

Friedberg, J.P., S. Suchday, and V.S. Srinivas. 2009. "Relationship Between Forgiveness and Psychological and Physiological Indices in Cardiac Patients." *International Journal of Behavioral Medicine* 16: 205–211.

Gandhi, M.K. 2000. *The Collected Works of Mahatma Gandhi. Vol.51.* New Delhi: Publications Division Ministry of Information and Broadcasting, Government of India.

Gilbert, P. 2009. "Introducing Compassion-Focused Therapy." *Advances in Psychiatric Treatment* 15: 199–208.

Goldstein, J. 2007. *A Heart Full of Peace.* Boston: Wisdom Publications.

Hanson, R. 2013. *Hardwiring Happiness: The New Brain Science of Contentment, Calm, and Confidence.* New York: Harmony Books.

Hanson, R., and R. Mendius. 2009. *Buddha's Brain: The Practical Neuroscience of Happiness, Love, and Wisdom.* Oakland, CA: New Harbinger Publications.

Harris, A.H.S., F. Luskin, S.B. Norman, S. Standard, J. Bruning, S. Evans, and C.E. Thoresen. 2006. "Effects of a Group Forgiveness Intervention on Forgiveness, Perceived Stress, and Trait-Anger." *Journal of Clinical Psychology* 62: 715–733.

Hasenkamp, W., C.Wilson-Mendenhall, E. Duncan, and L. Barsalou. 2012. "Mind Wandering and Attention During Focused Meditation: A Fine-Grained Temporal Analysis of Fluctuating Cognitive States." *NeuroImage* 59: 750–60.

Ilibagiza, I. 2006. *Left to Tell: Discovering God Amidst the Rwandan Holocaust.* With S. Erwin. Carlsbad, CA: Hay House.

James, W. 1890. *The Principles of Psychology, Vol.1.* New York: Henry Holt and Co.

Kabat-Zinn, J. 2005. *Coming to Our Senses: Healing Ourselves and the World Through Mindfulness.* New York: Hyperion.

Kabat-Zinn, J. 2013. *Full Catastrophe Living: Using the Wisdom of Your Body and Mind to Face Stress, Pain, and Illness.* Rev. ed. New York: Bantam.

Kemeny, M.E., C.Foltz, J.F. Cavanagh, M. Cullen, J. Giese-Davis, P. Jennings, et al. 2012. "Contemplative/Emotion Training Reduces Negative

Emotional Behavior and Promotes Prosocial Responses." *Emotion* 12: 338–50.

Killingsworth, M.A., and D.T. Gilbert. 2010. "A Wandering Mind Is an Unhappy Mind." *Science* 330: 932.

King, M.L. 1983. *The Words of Martin Luther King, Jr.* Edited by Coretta Scott King. New York: Newmarket Press.

Kornfield, J. "Changing My Mind, Year After Year." Jack Kornfield. November 5, 2012. http://www.jackkornfield.com/changing-my-mind-year-after-year

Ladinsky, D.J. 2010. *A Year with Hafiz: Daily Contemplations.* New York: Penguin Books.

Legault, L., T. Al-Khindi, and M. Inzlicht. 2012. "Preserving Integrity in the Face of Performance Threat: Self-Affirmation Enhances Neurophysiological Responsiveness to Errors." *Psychological Science* 23: 1455–60.

Logel, C., and G.L. Cohen. 2012. "The Role of the Self in Physical Health." *Psychological Science* 23: 53–55.

Longfellow, H.W. 2000. *Poems and Other Writings.* New York: Literary Classics of the United States.

Mann, T., A.J. Tomiyama, E. Westling, A.M. Lew, B. Samuels, and J. Chatman. 2007. "Medicare's Search for Effective Obesity Treatments: Diets Are Not the Answer." *American Psychologist* 62: 220–33.

Maslow, A.H. 1966. *The Psychology of Science; A Reconnaissance.* New York: Harper and Row.

Neff, K.D. 2011. *Self-Compassion: Stop Beating Yourself Up and Leave Insecurity Behind.* New York: William Morrow.

Neff, K.D., Y.P. Hsieh, and K. Dejitterat. 2005. "Self-Compassion, Achievement Goals, and Coping with Academic Failure." *Self and Identity* 4: 263–87.

Nhat Hanh, Thich. 1987. *The Miracle of Mindfulness: An Introduction to the Practice of Meditation.* Translated by M. Ho. Boston: Beacon Press.

Nhat Hanh, Thich. 1997. *Stepping into Freedom: An Introduction to Buddhist Monastic Training.* Berkeley, CA: Parallax Press.

Nhat Hanh, Thich. 2004. *True Love: A Practice for Awakening the Heart.* Translated by S. Chödzin. Boston: Shambhala.

NHLBI (National Heart, Lung, and Blood Institute). 2003. *National Sleep Disorders Research Plan.* Bethesda, MD: National Institutes of Health.

Nisker, W. 2008. *Crazy Wisdom Saves the World Again! Handbook for a Spiritual Revolution.* Berkeley, CA: Stone Bridge Press.

Rilke, R.M. 1984. *Letters to a Young Poet.* Translated by S. Mitchell. New York: Random House.

Roeser, R.W., K.A. Schonert-Reichl, A. Jha, M. Cullen, L. Wallace, R. Wilensky, E. Oberle, K. Thomson, C. Taylor, and J. Harrison. 2013. "Mindfulness Training and Reductions in Teacher Stress and Burnout: Results from Two Randomized, Waitlist-Control Field Trials." *Journal of Educational Psychology* 105: 787–804.

Rogers, C.R. 1957. "The Necessary and Sufficient Conditions of Therapeutic Personality Change." *Journal of Consulting Psychology* 21: 95–103.

Rosenberg, M.B. 2003. *Nonviolent Communication: A Language of Life.* 2nd ed. Encinitas, CA: PuddleDancer Press.

Salzberg, S. 2004. "The Power of Intention." *The Oprah Magazine,* January 2004. http://www.oprah.com/spirit/Sharon-Salzberg-The-Power-of-Intention

Schmeichel, B.J., and K. Vohs. 2009. "Self-Affirmation and Self-Control: Affirming Core Values Counteracts Ego Depletion." *Journal of Personality and Social Psychology* 96: 770–82.

Shapiro, F.R. 2006. *The Yale Book of Quotations.* New Haven: Yale University Press.

Stoia-Caraballo, R., M.S. Rye, W. Pan, K.J.B. Kirschman, C. Lutz-Zois, and A.M. Lyons. 2008. "Negative Affect and Anger Rumination as Mediators Between Forgiveness and Sleep Quality." *Journal of Behavioral Medicine* 31: 478–88.

Thondup, T. 1988. *The Healing Power of Mind: Simple Meditation Exercises for Health, Well-Being, and Enlightenment.* Boston: Shambhala.

Tolstoy, L. 2008. *Anna Karenina.* Auckland: Floating Press.

Trungpa, C. 1999. *The Essential Chögyam Trungpa.* Edited by C.R. Gimian. Boston: Shambhala.

Trungpa, C. 2003. *The Collected Works of Chögyam Trungpa. Volume 2.* Edited by C.R. Gimian. Boston: Shambhala.

Turan, B., C. Foltz, J. Cavanagh, A. Wallace, M. Cullen, E. Rosenberg, P. Jennings, P. Ekman, and M. Kemeny. 2015. "Anticipatory Sensitization to Repeated Stressors: The Role of Initial Cortisol Reactivity and Meditation/Emotion Skills Training." *Psychoneuroendocrinology* 52: 229–38.

Tutu, D. 1999. *No Future Without Forgiveness.* New York: Doubleday.

Wang, Z., and J.M. Tchernev. 2012. "The 'Myth' of Media Multitasking: Reciprocal Dynamics of Media Multitasking, Personal Needs, and Gratifications." *Journal of Communication* 62: 493–513.

Whyte, D. 2002. *The Heart Aroused: Poetry and the Preservation of the Soul in Corporate America.* New York: Doubleday.

Williams, J.G., S.K. Stark, and E.E. Foster. 2008. "Start Today or the Very Last Day?—The Relationships Among Self-Compassion, Motivation, and Procrastination." *American Journal of Psychological Research* 4: 37–44.

Margaret Cullen, MA, MFT, is a licensed marriage and family therapist and a certified mindfulness-based stress reduction (MBSR) teacher. She has also trained with Zindel Segal in mindfulness-based cognitive therapy. For over twenty years she has been teaching and pioneering mindfulness programs in a variety of settings, including cancer support, HIV support, physician groups, executive groups, and obesity support. For ten years she has been involved in teaching and writing curricula for several research programs at the University of California, San Francisco, including "Cultivating Emotional Balance," designed for teachers, and "Craving and Lifestyle Management with Meditation," for overweight women. In 2008 she launched a mindfulness-based emotional balance program for teachers and school administrators that has been piloted in Denver, CO; Boulder, CO; Ann Arbor, MI; Berkeley, CA; Portland, OR; and Vancouver, BC. She has also been a facilitator of support groups for cancer patients and their loved ones for twenty-five years at the Cancer Support Community, and is currently a senior teacher at the Center for Compassion and Altruism Research and Education at Stanford University, where she contributed to the *Compassion Cultivation* training manual. A longtime contributor to *Inquiring Mind,* Margaret has been a meditation practitioner for 35 years.

Gonzalo Brito Pons, PhD, is a clinical psychologist who has worked with diverse populations in Chile, Peru, and Spain, integrating Western psychological approaches with traditional medicine and contemplative practices. As a certified yoga teacher and mindfulness-based stress reduction (MBSR) instructor, he has included these practices in his clinical work and workshops for health care professionals and educators over the last decade. Gonzalo is a certified instructor of the Compassion Cultivation Training Program and serves as a supervisor for Spanish-speaking teachers in training at the Center for Compassion and Altruism Research and Education at Stanford University. He obtained his PhD doing experimental research on the individual and relational effects of compassion cultivation training and mindfulness-based stress reduction. Currently living in Granada, Spain, Gonzalo combines his therapeutic work with ongoing compassion-based and mindfulness-based programs, collaborating regularly with several educational and health organizations. In 2014, he coauthored the book *Presencia plena: Reflexiones y prácticas para cultivar mindfulness en la vida diaria* (Full presence: Reflections and practices to cultivate mindfulness in daily life).

Foreword writer **Jon Kabat-Zinn, PhD,** is internationally known for his work as a scientist, writer, and meditation teacher engaged in bringing mindfulness into the mainstream of medicine and society. He is professor of medicine emeritus at the University of Massachusetts Medical School, and author of numerous books, including *Full Catastrophe Living,*

Arriving at Your Own Door, and *Coming to Our Senses.*

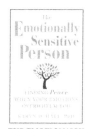

Register your **new harbinger** titles for additional benefits!

When you register your **new harbinger** title—purchased in any format, from any source—you get access to benefits like the following:

- Downloadable accessories like printable worksheets and extra content
- Instructional videos and audio files
- Information about updates, corrections, and new editions

Not every title has accessories, but we're adding new material all the time.

Access free accessories in 3 easy steps:

1. Sign in at NewHarbinger.com (or **register** to create an account).

2. Click on **register a book**. Search for your title and click the **register** button when it appears.

3. Click on the **book cover or title** to go to its details page. Click on **accessories** to view and access files.

That's all there is to it!

If you need help, visit:

NewHarbinger.com/accessories

new harbinger
CELEBRATING
40 YEARS

Back Cover Material

YOUR GUIDE TO CULTIVATING EMOTIONAL BALANCE

Experiencing emotions is a part of the richness of life. But sometimes emotions can get in the way of our health and happiness. Suppressing strong feelings like fear, anger, and resentment isn't the answer—in fact, doing so can lead to host of physical problems, from a weakened immune system to heart disease. On the other hand, overreacting in the heat of the moment can be detrimental to relationships. So, how can you ride even the strongest waves of emotion without causing harm to yourself or others?

This workbook offers a breakthrough, eight-week program using emotion theory and mindfulness-based techniques to help you manage the overwhelming thoughts and feelings that cause you pain. You'll learn to approach your emotions without judgment, understand their source, and foster forgiveness and kindness toward both yourself and others. Instead of trying to bury feelings or lashing out and hurting relationships, you'll learn how to cultivate emotional balance using this powerful program.

"This wise and practical book is filled with wonderful practices that can regulate your emotions and change your life."
—Jack Kornfield, PhD, author of *The Wise Heart*

"This pragmatic and wise workbook provides readers with clearsighted guidance for self-care when distressing effects loom."
—Zindel V. Segal. PhD, distinguished professor of psychology in mood disorders, University of Toronto Scarborough

Margaret Cullen, MA, MIFT, is a licensed marriage and family therapist and a certified mindfulness-based stress reduction teacher. For over twenty years she has been teaching and pioneering mindfulness programs in a variety of settings.

Gonzalo Brito Pons, PhD, is a psychologist who has worked with diverse populations in Chile, Peru, and Spain, integrating western psychological approaches with local traditional medicine. Along with his therapeutic work, he regularly teaches mindfulness and compassion cultivation programs.

Foreword writer **Jon Kabat-Zinn, PhD,** is internationally known for his work as a scientist, writer, and meditation teacher engaged in bringing mindfulness into the mainstream of medicine and society. He is author of *Full Catastrophe Living.*